Contents

BASILEA SCHLINK, born in 1904, was the founder of the Evangelical Sisterhood of Mary, an interdenominational Christian ministry based in Germany, with branches in eleven countries. She was the author of more than one hundred books with translations in more than sixty languages. Mother Basilea went home to the Lord in 2001.

I

"I Have This Against You..."

Has the Word of God in Revelation 2:4 ever halted you in your tracks? Have you ever felt a strange uneasiness that pierced to the heart as you read these words: "I have this against you, that you have abandoned the love you had at first"?

This was my experience during a time when I was fully occupied with the work of God's Kingdom. Every moment seemed to be taken up with God's work: youth groups, teaching missions, Bible classes, private counseling; much of this required detailed preparation, and often left me on the brink of exhaustion. It was during World War II. The suffering, both physical and spiritual, created in many German people a hunger for the Word of God. They filled the churches and parish halls for my lectures. They received the Word of God with thankful hearts, as the many letters and comments testified. Time simply would not stretch to cover all the requests for Bible studies and lectures that came from churches and groups throughout Germany.

Wouldn't you expect that such a response to one's ministry

would delight the heart? Indeed, I was thankful for the privilege of this ministry for Jesus. Besides this, my personal life was a joy: I lived with a friend with whom I could share both my inner life and the prayer and burden for my work.

What could be missing from this full life in God's service? Didn't it all revolve around Jesus? I thought so.

But then came a moment when a word from God unsettled me. I can't remember now whether it was through hearing and reading the Bible, or during prayer. It was this word about "abandoning your first love." With this word of Scripture, a dark question mark suddenly rose up to cloud my own faith and my service for Jesus. I read on a few verses—the sharp judgment of Jesus over the leader of the Church in Ephesus. Did Jesus speak this same sharp judgment over me? Did He also say to me: "Remember then from what you have fallen, repent" (v. 5). How was it with my "first love"? I didn't fully grasp what the Scripture meant by "first love." But one thing I knew: my own love toward Jesus was a sham.

I thought back to the time when the living God came into my life in a definite way. Was it not indeed "another love" which then burned in my heart? Had I traded this love toward Jesus— traded it for a love of my ministry, which so filled my days and satisfied my heart?

This can be a subtle thing. Read the Lord's message to the Church in Ephesus, in Revelation *2:* "I know your works, your toil and your patient endurance, and how you cannot bear evil men but have tested those who call themselves apostles but are not, and found them to be false; I know you are enduring patiently and bearing up for my name's sake, and you have not grown weary" (vv. 2, 3). Much to approve! Much to praise! He separates himself from evil men, he endures patiently through testings and difficulties, he has not grown weary. Surely here is

a spiritual leader who has the right love toward Jesus.

Yet the very next verse brings this sharp retort of Jesus: "I have this against you, that you have abandoned the love you had at first." As I studied this, I became more and more unsettled. If the "first love" is not any of the things which Jesus praises in this leader of the Church at Ephesus—and my own ministry was no match for his—then what exactly *is* it, and why does Jesus value it so highly?

It disturbed me that Jesus threatened to "remove your lampstand from its place" (v. 5). Here was a seemingly vital, healthy church (which of ours could compare with it?), yet Jesus was ready to cut it off, simply because He did not find there this "first love."

My whole ministry lay under a cloud. For I saw one thing clearly: no matter how praiseworthy our ministry may be, it will in the end fall under judgment if this "first love" be wanting. Truly, something basic and decisive hangs upon our abiding in this "first love." God has set great value upon it. Further, I realized that without this "first love" we cannot expect to bring forth real fruit, nor can we be prepared to participate in the glory of the Marriage Supper of the Lamb. To attain to this, at any cost, was my deepest longing.

What did the Lord mean by the "first love"? Why did its loss cause Him such great pain? The answer came, at last, in prayer. It came through I Corinthians 13.

The immediate question in this chapter of Scripture has to do with love toward one's neighbor. The distinctive feature of the love here portrayed is that it always seeks other people. It is not a love motivated by heroism or idealism—which might "give away all I have, and . . . deliver my body to be burned" (v. 3), yet at root, even though unrecognized, have the expression of my own ego in view. This was my key. Now I saw what Jesus

meant by the "first love." Now I grasped what He was asking of those who believed in Him, in Revelation 2. It had to do with love which seeks nothing for itself. Yet it moved beyond a love which seeks other people. For this "first love" seeks not people, but a Person, the One who alone merits our *first* love. The "first love" is the intimate personal relationship of love which one has with our Lord Jesus Christ.

Now the Spirit of God threw His spotlight upon my life. True enough, I had believed in Jesus as my Lord and Saviour. I had accepted Him by faith. Out of love, I had dedicated myself to His service. My life stood at His disposal. I was His witness. And yet—and *yet!* At first it passed scarcely noticed. But with the passing of the years, little by little, this love had ebbed away—this "first love," which alone could satisfy Jesus.

One might see a comparison in the relationship of a wife to her husband. She once gave him her love freely, for his own sake. The years intervene. In the marriage she still serves him faithfully. She has a care for his needs. She even shares fully with him the responsibility and burden of the family business. Yet the husband knows that something is missing. The intimate, personal tie to him is not the same as it was in the days of their first love. She no longer shows a desire to be alone with him. She avoids the opportunities to draw close to him. At the first her time was his, but no more. Now she is just as happy to give her time to work. Indeed, she gives herself wholly to her work, though she tells herself it is "all for him."

I came to see that my relationship to my Lord Jesus Christ, with the passing years, had eroded away something like a marriage gone humdrum. What did I do when I found a little pocket of spare time, on a Sunday or a holiday? I couldn't wait to get together with other people—people I liked, people with whom I had something in common—so we could share ideas and expe-

riences. Or I read a stimulating book. Or I went out to enjoy nature. I even plunged further into my work, doing things that I normally didn't have time for. But to go to Jesus—to give Him first claim on even my spare time—that I did not do. My love was a divided love. It belonged as much to some other person, or to the particular thing I was interested in, as to Jesus. In holding a regular "Quiet Time," my purpose was not to seek the quiet of prayer, where the love between Jesus and me might find expression. I had no desire to be much alone with Him. I did not want to hear the concerns which weigh on His heart. I had no deep longing to make Him happy. My thoughts wandered here and there, when they were not directly focused upon some subject. And so also did my feet: as soon as I had a free moment, I was off and going—but never to some quiet place of prayer. Yet it was there that Jesus was waiting for me.

True love, however, seeks the loved one out. That is what Jesus does. For He is love, as the Scripture says, "God is love" (I John 4:8). He seeks us out. Yet He waits for our love in turn to seek Him out. He waits for a love which seeks Him and Him alone. Nothing can satisfy the heart of Jesus except our love.

It is important that we dedicate ourselves unstintingly to our work. It is important that we bear our burdens with patience. It is important that we hate evil, and tolerate no compromise with it. Such things will always be necessary for a Christian. But such things alone do not satisfy Jesus. He wants more. He wants the intimate, personal surrender of our hearts to Him. Not just once, when we first experience the grace of forgiveness and salvation. No, He wants them ever and again—new every morning.

This is the truth which broke in upon my life, as I read the Lord's message to the Church at Ephesus, in Revelation 2. For here our love to Jesus is not equated with a generalized notion of "love to God." (Often we have only the haziest notion of love

toward God; it is, as it were, one love among many, jostling for recognition within our hearts.) No, in these words to the Church at Ephesus, Jesus' meaning is unmistakably clear: He means a love without parallel, truly the "first love."

As I prayed over this, the clouds of uncertainty and confusion began to lift. I began to see that here one and only one kind of love could be meant: bridal love. For it is just here—in the love of a bride for her bridegroom—that we speak in this way of a "first love." Through the picture of a bride's love, we could come to a deeper understanding of what Jesus means by the "first love."

A sadness crept through my heart as I thought about a bride's "first love." For this love has a distinctive characteristic: it has eyes for the bridegroom alone. He alone fills her every thought, her every moment; to him alone goes the yearning of her heart. When I observed my own love to Jesus, such a yearning, such an absoluteness seemed utterly lacking. Bridal love is all-your-eggs-in-one-basket love. It gives up all others. Bridal love is a spendthrift love, lavish love, doesn't-count-the-cost love. It does foolish things. Bridal love is sacrificial love. It gives everything to the beloved. All of this—all that would truly characterize love as bridal love—one would search in vain to find in my love to Jesus.

Deeper and deeper went the sword of God's Word. The Spirit of God convicted me that I had indeed lost this one thing, this most important of all things, this that meant everything to Jesus—my "first love," my personal, intimate love to Jesus. Perhaps I had even prided myself, in years past, that my Christianity was so disciplined and controlled, and therefore concluded everything was in order. Like many Christians I had assumed that we gradually lose the love we have at first for the Lord. I thought it fades away—just as in a good marriage—to be replaced by a

reasoned, mature love that is more sober, realistic, and down-to-earth. This was the delusion I was living under.

But now the scales fell from my eyes. Precisely on the point of being soberly realistic, my love to Jesus had failed. My sin stood naked and exposed in the light of God's Word: I had not taken the command of Jesus seriously. For He had called for a love that sets Him above everything, that loves Him with all our might, that devotes to Him everything that we are and have. Who is truly realistic and sober in his love? Only he who holds to his "first love"—spendthrift love, foolish love. This was now clear to me, for only such a love is obedient to the First Commandment.

Can one actually do "too much" when it comes to love toward Jesus? Can one measure out love toward One whose love is beyond measure? Yet that was what I had done. And why? Because I was no longer in the thrall of His love, no longer circled about with His glory and beauty. Therefore my love had grown cold. Therefore the word of Scripture stood as a judgment over my life: "You have abandoned your first love."

Heartsick, I began to long for the renewal of this "first love." And not only to long for it, but to pray and beseech God for it. I knew that I must have this love, no matter what the cost. For the alternative was clear: to be left standing outside a closed door at the Marriage Supper of the Lamb. I must abide in this love. Otherwise all my service for Jesus would come under judgment. My lampstand would be removed. He would cast me away like an unfruitful branch, to be burned, because I had not remained in His love, as the branch abides in the vine. Now I saw clearly: life depends upon love. If our "life" is to beget life in others, it must be a life bound in love to Jesus.

As my longing and my prayers for this love grew stronger, I came to see why I had lost this "first love," and why I now sought it with such longing. First of all, my heart was divided. I

did not love Jesus with my whole heart. But besides this, another great barrier lay across my path: self-righteousness. So I began to pray that the Lord would humble me, and give me a broken heart. I thought of the woman in Luke 7 who had sinned much. She fell weeping at Jesus' feet. Then, out of thankfulness for His gift of forgiveness, her great love poured out. I prayed for this kind of repentance—and love.

The Lord answered my prayer. He always answers petitions which are in accord with His will—and the prayer for a contrite heart is always according to His will. In the following years He led me through many humbling, difficult judgments and disciplines. I learned to weep over my sins. In spirit, I fell at the feet of both men and God, as a helpless sinner. I humbled myself in repentance before people I had sinned against. And in the measure that I accepted these judgments, God granted me a personal love to our Lord.

Since I have learned to love Jesus, my life has become unspeakably rich and happy. In Him is fullness of contentment. What a privilege: to love Him of Whose love it is written, "How fair and how pleasant art thou, O love, for delights!" (Song of Solomon 7:6 KJV). No more could suffering and the cross come upon me as an oppressive power. For now I had learned to go the way of the cross. His love to me, and mine to Him, transformed the cross.

In the measure that my love to Jesus grew, people and the things of this world became unimportant; they no longer held me in bondage. In this sense I could understand the words of the apostle John: "Do not love the world or the things in the world" (I John 2:15). More and more I became independent of anything the world could give or take away. Jesus became everything to me.

The portals of heaven opened wider and wider. The glory of

heaven shone forth. Should one not expect just that, as the Scripture says: ". . . seek the things that are above, where Christ is . . ." (Colossians 3:1). Jesus lives in heaven. If you seek Him, you will find Him there, at the right hand of God. And finding Him, you will find all heaven!

But not only did heaven come to me: the earth, also, came as a new gift. For both heaven and earth belong to Him. A bride must love everything that belongs to the bridegroom. The soul who loves Jesus loves everything that is His—heaven and earth, His creation, all His creatures which He surrounds with His love and care, especially mankind, for whom He gave His life, and above all the "brethren," those who belong to His Body, the Church. Nor does the Bride's love stop here. It goes on and learns from Jesus to love also her enemies—those who oppose Him or us.

"First love"—can any gift compare with it? What greater wish could one desire? Truly, in this, one has a foretaste of heaven here on earth. One is borne on the wings of this love toward the heavenly glory which God has prepared for those who love Him—the Marriage Supper of the Lamb.

What follows in this little book is drawn out of personal experience. It will say again, in differing ways, what we have said already: that a bridal love to Jesus must be the Alpha and Omega of our life. How blessed it is to love Jesus!

2

Jesus' Love Toward Us– Love Beyond Measure

The "first love," indeed all love to Jesus, springs from His love: ". . . he first loved us" (I John 4:19) And who is this One who has bestowed His love upon the children of men? Who is He? He is more than any heart can grasp, more than any mind can comprehend. The Psalmist says of Him, "You are the fairest of the sons of men" (Psalm 45:2). He is the son of God. He reflects the glory of God. His radiance illumines the New Jerusalem, for ". . . its lamp is the Lamb" (Revelation 21:23). He upholds the universe by His word of power. He bears the very stamp of God's nature. So glorious and majestic is Jesus, that all the angels worship and adore Him. So great and mighty are His works, that the entire universe was created by Him (Hebrews 1:1–6). Indeed, He is the King of Kings, and Lord of Lords!

Yet behold Him again, this King and Lord! See Him humble and lowly. He leaves the glory of heaven. He comes to the sons of men, to sinners. They do not want Him, and they will not receive Him. Yet He comes. He takes on their flesh and blood.

He walks among them. ". . . He is not ashamed to call them brethren" (Hebrews 2:11). He created them in love. They hated Him in return. Yet He loves them still. In the end they torture Him to death. They deride and mock. They nail Him to a cross. He loves them.

Again and again, His words toward them are words of love and compassion. His is a foolish love. A spendthrift love that lavishes love upon those who trample Him under foot. It offers everything.

He had but to speak a word, and all His enemies would have fallen prostrate before Him. What a foolhardy love! All manner of hatred and evil spewed out against Him, and still He has but one answer: love. He can do nothing but love. For He has lost His heart to the children of men.

To this day it remains the same. We do not return His love. We disappoint His love. We abandon His love. Yet He loves us still. Suffering, He loves on. As He loved His disciples, though they deserted Him; His people, though they rejected Him. So does He continue to love us . . . until His love has reclaimed us. He lives, that He may love us.

His entire nature is compassed in the one word: love. Love interprets all His words, for they are spoken out of a heart that loves. Love streams forth from His countenance like the noonday sun. The wounds in His hands, His feet, and His side speak again of love. His love led Him to suffer. His human children languished in chains of darkness, prisoners of Satan. Through suffering He rescued them, that He might again enfold them in His love, in His kingdom of blessedness.

In heaven Jesus sits upon His throne. But He does not possess this royal glory for Himself alone; He shares His praise, His kingdom, and His power with us. Though we were His enemies, His love wants us at His side . . . for He *is* love. When He had

made His life a sacrifice unto death, He arose and took His place at the right hand of the majesty on high. There He waits. In patience—and in love—He waits until all His enemies are brought to His feet. His love can only be satisfied by our love, freely given. He does not stomp His enemies under foot, forcing them to bow down and pay Him homage. He waits.

More than a man would ever wait—differently than a man would ever wait—He waits for our love. For we were brought forth from Him. The Bible says, ". . . we are members of his body" (Ephesians 5:30). We were created and redeemed that we might respond to His love, giving Him our love in return. Human beings might wait awhile for our love. Then suddenly they wait no longer. They wheel about and find someone else to love. But it is not so with our Lord Jesus. His love is unfathomable. He can only wait for our love. Humanly speaking, we are His "one and only." And so He waits. Patiently. Humbly. Until finally He hears from those whom He redeemed with His Blood an answering echo of love. The "first love." The bridal love.

Jesus' love stands alone. No other can love as He loves. In no human love will you find the intense glow and power that you find in Jesus' love. In no human love will you discover the depth and tenderness of our Lord Jesus. The most tender love of a bridegroom, the deepest love of a mother, is but a pale shadow of His love, for indeed such love finds its source in His love. No father, no mother, no bridegroom is so inventive and alert in love, bestowing blessing and good upon the beloved, as is Jesus. Do we really grasp what it means—to be loved by Jesus, the Son of man, King and Lord, the Bridegroom and Friend of our soul? His love truly gives them to drink from the river of his delights (Psalm 36:8). He blesses a human life with His love, as no human could.

St. Francis of Assisi demonstrated through his own life what

a power of blessing lay in this love of Jesus. One sees it already in the report of his conversion, then again and again throughout his life:

Francis of Assisi, twenty-three years old, chosen leader of a club, one evening put on a lavish banquet, as he had often done before. Afterward they wound their way, singing, through the town. Francis held aloft a staff, symbol of the leader. Then all at once Francis fell a little behind the others. He no longer sang. He sank into his thoughts. For in that moment the Lord had touched him. A sweetness flooded his heart, such a sweetness that he could neither speak nor move. He could feel nothing but that sweetness. Nothing else seemed real. . . . The others looked back at him, for he had now fallen some distance behind. They turned around and started back toward him. As they drew closer, their eyes widened in amazement: it was as though Francis was transformed into another person.

"What's gotten into you?" one of them asked.

"What's the matter? Why aren't you coming along? Did you see a girl—some girl you want to see home?"

"Yes, that is it," he answered, a strange vibrancy coming into his voice. "And what a beauty she is! For the damsel I was thinking about, whom I want to see home, is nobler and richer and lovelier than any you have ever seen!"

They laughed at him. But he had not said this of himself; it came by divine inspiration. For his "damsel" was the true worship and adoration of God. To this damsel he would surrender himself. She was nobler, richer, and lovelier in her poverty than any other woman in the midst of splendor. . . .

This was the "pearl of great price." To obtain her, Francis would sell everything he had. And because he wanted

to protect her from the gaze of the scoffers, he would go often, indeed daily, to the quiet of prayer, drawn by the sweetness of Jesus. (from *FRANCIS OF ASSISI, Legends and Tales,* by Otto Karrer)

Jesus not only slakes our thirst with the sweetness and the delights of His love. He goes further. He comforts and refreshes us with His love in the midst of suffering, where human love can no longer comfort and refresh us. When Jesus comes, shedding abroad His love, desperation is transformed into joy. Though we languished in the very depths of suffering, Jesus could transform it into a foretaste of heaven by His presence.

I am reminded of an unusually difficult year in my life. One of my spiritual daughters came to an early death, after some months of pain and agony. I had taken her into my innermost heart. Her suffering came near to breaking my heart. How I had prayed and believed that the Lord would touch her!

Some few months later another of our young sisters came to the doorstep of death; she had incurred a severe illness in wartime service. We were very close. She had borne with me all the burdens of the Sisterhood. Again it meant standing for long weeks at the bedside of a beloved "daughter," bearing her pain and torment in my own heart, yet not able to help. And again God answered our prayers with silence. He gave her into the hands of death. He called her home, this one still so young. Nor was His time of discipline past. The weeks of strain and suffering took their toll, and I myself fell deathly ill. Besides all this, the work of our Sisterhood at this time faced seemingly insurmountable obstacles.

Humanly speaking, everything looked dark. We were about to bury our second spiritual daughter. Because we had been so close, her death had been a particularly hard blow. Yet just at

this time, I experienced how Jesus can comfort one whom He loves.

The coffin stood in our chapel. I lay weak and sick in bed. The difficulties facing our Sisterhood rose up like great waves before me. Sadness weighed like a great stone on my heart.

Then Jesus drew near and said, "I will come to you." I did not see Him with my eyes. Yet His presence was unmistakably real. His love flooded my heart, filling it with joy and comfort. Palpably He caused me to know what happens when He draws near us in love—our hearts are refreshed, and our spirits are brought back from despair. In the midst of deepest suffering, heaven opened and bent low to meet me in my need—something of heaven's joy broke in upon my grief.

The funeral was no ordinary funeral. Both in the chapel and by the graveside, it was filled with songs of the Resurrection and of heaven. Afterwards, many people said they had never before experienced such a funeral: the joy of heaven so breathed upon it that sadness and grief melted away.

Yes, sadness and grief do melt away under the power of Jesus' comforting love. Many have known and testified to this heavenly reality—even through terms in concentration camps and prisons, which of themselves were a foretaste of hell. Where a loving heart opens up and receives the presence of Jesus, there heaven becomes reality, for the essence of heaven is to come into the presence of Jesus. Where He comes to us as the Lord of love, everything becomes light, for He is the light of the world. When His face shines upon us, we are healed of our griefs and sorrows.

We know how a person in suffering will take comfort from the smile, even the glance, of a loved one. Indeed, in the loved one the sufferer sees a beauty beside which everything else pales. One will freely give up money and goods, house and

friends—give up everything—if only he may feast upon the sight of the loved one.

No countenance can compare in beauty with the countenance of Jesus. It is like the sun for brightness. When we dwell upon it, a deep and quiet charm steals into our hearts. The clouds of suffering lift. It stirs in one a love a thousand times more powerful than any human love. For this love, one counts "everything as loss" (Philippians 3:8).

Do we sinful human beings truly grasp the immensity of His grace? Jesus inclines His heart toward us. From this heart, the heart of Jesus, we are overwhelmed with love. And this is the same heart which is the center of the universe, the ground of everything that exists. From this heart goes forth a stream of love that quickens and sustains the life of the whole world.

Think what it means to have another human being open his heart to you. Imagine further that it is a person of great station and honor, one altogether lovely and charming. If this be desirable, what then must it mean when Jesus opens His heart to us? Yes, to gaze into the heart that is naught but love itself! This is the blessedness and rapture of one to whom Jesus opens His heart!

Who can praise enough the love of our Lord Jesus? Sadly, we praise it but little, for we have come to know it but little. For there is a price to pay, if you would know Jesus' love: you must surrender to Him your whole heart, as He Himself says, ". . . he who loves me . . . I will love . . . and [I will] manifest myself to him" (John 14:21).

What does the love of Jesus bring us? There is no measuring it. It goes beyond all human standards. The most priceless treasure in heaven and earth is the heart of God, and His love to us.

Our longing and desire—in this world and in the world to come—should pursue this alone: to obtain the love of Jesus, to be loved by Him, to have His loving heart revealed to us, and to love Him in turn.

3

Our Love Toward Jesus–
Our FIRST Love?

We have seen something of *Jesus'* love—radiant and beautiful, noble and majestic, deep and gentle, burning and powerful. What of our love toward Him? Can a sinful human being even respond to such a love? We are tempted to think that it cannot be possible—and yet it is. For God created us in His own image. He chose us to be His friends. Think a moment how He called Abraham and Moses "my friend" (Isaiah 41:8, Exodus 33:11). God has chosen us for the most intimate fellowship of love with Himself. Think again how He spoke of His chosen people, Israel, in these words: ". . . as a bridegroom rejoices over the bride, so shall your God rejoice over you" (Isaiah 62:5). Jesus came to redeem us that we might fulfill this calling, and experience the truth of God's Word: "I will betroth you to me forever" (Hosea 2:19). He came so the Spirit of God might pour His love into our hearts. He came so the flame of His love might kindle an answering love in our hearts—a love that sets everything at naught in order to return the fire of His love.

Consider the "exclusiveness" of purely human love. A girl's whole life is focused on her beloved. She has eyes and ears only for him. She gives him her whole heart. How much more must this be true of our love toward Jesus!

Mary Magdalene offers us an example. She is one who had an overflowing love for Jesus. Before Jesus' love broke in upon her life, she had "loved" many men. After she met Jesus, she turned her back on all these "loves." She gave her heart to Jesus alone.

Her actions demonstrate how completely this love for Jesus possessed her. She heard that Jesus was in Simon's house. She rushed over there. She didn't stop to ask what the Pharisees might say. Didn't she know what an impossibility this was—that she, a woman, barge into a meeting of men, and men having a theological discussion at that? Couldn't she see how impossible her conduct would appear? She, a known sinner, walking right into the presence of the "Protectors of Religion and Morals"! Had she no premonition of the slander and reviling she would face? No, in her love she paid no regard to all of this. She had no thought except for Jesus. Everything that used to be important to her sank out of sight in His Presence. Thus Jesus could speak of her as one who "loved much" (Luke 7:47).

In Mary Magdalene we see the glow of "first love"—the love that sees nothing but Jesus, is interested in Him above everything else, and hastens to Him at every opportunity. Mary Magdalene wants Jesus Himself. She wants to be close to Him, ever in His presence. She wants to gaze into His face, for there she encounters His forgiving love. She wants to hear a word from His lips that speaks of His love and forgiveness. She does not mind the cost. To know the love of Jesus, to linger in His presence is her most priceless privilege. She pays no heed to the humiliation this may bring. She does not care that she may lose what little respect she had from other people, nor that she will lose the love of

those on whom she formerly squandered her love. Her heart now draws her to the One whom alone she has chosen to love.

Thus it was with Mary Magdalene on Easter morning. She was the first one who hastened to the grave, seeking Jesus. No angel could so dazzle her with the beauty and splendor of his appearance and capture her soul. The angel was unimportant to her. She was not concerned with him, but only with Him whom her soul loved, her Lord Jesus. Thus she turned from the angel and questioned one whom she supposed to be the gardener, "Where have you laid him?" When she did not find Him in the grave, she continued to look. Love does not cease, for love continues to hope and believe even when all hope and expectation seems dead.

Love will not die. Love sets itself one goal, and will not surrender it: to know the beloved, and to be with Him. Nothing else can satisfy love. Compared to the beloved, all else is empty and worthless. Mary Magdalene could not rest until she could fall at Jesus' feet. He spoke her name—"Mary"—and her love answered—"Rabboni!"

Love for Jesus has an absolute quality about it. But for that very reason it has redemptive power. It breaks every bondage that has fettered us to men and to things. The love of Mary Magdalene focused upon Jesus alone. She, in turn, received Jesus completely, because she gave herself to Him without reservation. Mary Magdalene discovered the secret: you love Jesus absolutely, or you love Him not at all. She had responded according to the Word of God,

Hear, O daughter, consider, and incline your ear;
  forget your people and your father's house;
  and the king will desire your beauty.
Since he is your lord, bow to him.
  —Psalm 45:10,11

This is bridal love. It has eyes for Jesus only. It forgets all else. It forsakes all else. It desires nothing else but that He may delight Himself in the beauty of His bride. It cannot but fall down and worship Him.

This is love that has eyes and ears for One only. Her feet guide her to Him. Her hands are quick to serve Him. Her heart is stirred over and over again by the wonder of who He is, and her lips speak it out. She is like the hymn writer who pens the words, "Jesus, Name above all names . . ." and then seemingly cannot find enough words to express his love and adoration: "Jesus best and dearest; fount of perfect love; holiest, tenderest, nearest, purest, sweetest . . ." True love must lovingly search out new names for the Beloved. Often it is just this that characterizes the prayers of some of the great saints who through the ages have expressed their love for Jesus. Before he entered the Franciscan Order, the later Brother Bernhard overheard St. Francis praying with fervent love just one sentence, over and over: "My God, my All!"

Our Sisterhood of Mary especially treasures one testimony to such a love for Jesus. It is the testimony which we saw in the life of Methodist Superintendent Riedinger, the spiritual father and cofounder of our Sisterhood. The duties of his office were many. He traveled a great deal, giving lectures, holding missions. He was in constant demand as a pastoral counselor. But one thing he always held as more important than all else: time for prayer, time for Jesus.

Once when his work load was unusually demanding, he remarked in conversation, "But I need at least two hours every morning for my Lord!" Often this meant that he would get up at 4:00 A.M. He was no longer in good health. The difficult post-war years and the constant pressure of his work had taken their toll. Yet the center and beginning point for all his work, indeed for

his entire life, was this daily 'conversation of love' with his Lord and Bridegroom. That alone supplied power for his ministry.

His Bible studies on "Bridal Love" reached many. But his life itself was the decisive testimony. His life of worship, his passionate desire to bring all possible honor and glory to Jesus led many into a deeper experience of Jesus' love. When we would share a time of worship with him, we were often shocked by the fervor of this love. It seemingly could not do enough to praise the attributes of the Beloved, to adore Him as Lamb and King, as High Priest and Bridegroom. And no day dared go by, in which the Beloved should wait in vain for his adoration.

This love of Pastor Riedinger, which wanted to see Jesus glorified, was the spark which kindled our own ministry of worship. It prepared the way for the ministry of our worship choirs.

Bridal love has one dominant characteristic: it occupies itself exclusively with Jesus, it is always available to Him, it finds complete fulfillment in Him. This quality of love gives a whole new direction to one's life. It takes the smallest elements of one's life, and relates them to Jesus.

I think of a young woman. She was beautiful, winsome, talented. A young man loved her, and she found her heart responding to his love. But then Jesus came to her. He came as the Bridegroom asking for all her love. She perceived in this the call to give her life exclusively to Him. The Scripture does point out to us that many are called to live to "please the Lord," and therefore do not enter into marriage (I Corinthians 7:32–38).

She responded to this call. She forsook everything that had made her life full and happy. She sought only Him. To offer herself in service to Him, as a Sister—this became the pulsebeat of her life. And she was happy, for she had found Jesus. Indeed, she so radiated joy that people said to one another: "If you want to see a really *happy* person, go and see that Sister!"

In the years that followed, her life became a testimony which kindled in many others this same "first love" toward Jesus. Her whole being and behavior testified to the matchless worth of Jesus' love. In her, people could see the happiness that comes from loving Jesus with an undivided heart, above all others. Loving Jesus bears endless fruit.

Again, I think of a deaconess. For long years she was in poor health. Yet through all the years of her service, decades long, she volunteered for night duty. It gave her greater opportunity to be in prayer with her Lord. Love seeks out such opportunities. She is the prayer warrior for her whole Mother House. The others could not imagine the Mother House without her. And many the Sisters who have found their way to this praying deaconess for spiritual counsel.

I think of a teacher. The school term left her exhausted and looking forward to some weeks of rest and recuperation. She planned a vacation in the mountains, eager for the bracing air, the warm sun. She bought her ticket. Everything was arranged with a friend who was going with her. But then she sensed: "Jesus is waiting for me! He wants my time—all my time! There will be no time because of all the activities and get-togethers I have planned—" She would not let her Lord wait in vain. She cancelled her plans. She had a time of quiet, and gave Jesus her vacation money. In these weeks she was more strengthened and returned to her work with greater joy than from any previous vacation.

This love, which sets Jesus above all else, finds unexpected applications in our everyday life—in places where we might least expect it.

A woman attended one of our retreats, and there experienced something of the love—and the suffering—of the living God. Moved by the experience, she said, "All my life I have had

a funny feeling about cleaning house on Friday. It just didn't seem right, but I didn't know why. Now I see: that is the day of our Lord's suffering. From now on, Friday can never be house-cleaning day. That must be a day of quiet and prayer, a day which I give my Lord. The housecleaning can well enough be done on other days."

These examples portray something of this love for Jesus—a love that sees only Him, lives for Him alone. And the character-istic by which you may recognize this love is this: it is prodigal; first love is a lavish, extravagant love. It is ready to lose and give up everything it has, down to its very last possession. Could it be otherwise? If we begin truly to love Jesus, could we think of care-fully measuring out our love—to Him whose love toward us is beyond measure? Can we put a price upon His great love for us? It is the price of death—His death for us, His enemies. What response is equal to such a love? Can it be anything less than a lavish, extravagant love that gives all, never counting the cost?

Our love to Jesus must outstrip all human loves. It must move us to sacrifice more of the goods and treasures of our life to Him than to any other person. For Jesus is our King. He it is who has lavished upon us His own great love, setting us free to love truly. It is His right to ask a devoted, extravagant love from His human children. True love for Jesus carries in its bosom a power—a power that grows out beyond itself. It cannot do otherwise than give to Him, without limit, never reckoning the cost. Those who so love lose every thought of holding back something for them-selves. They give up freely their possessions, their rights, their energy, their claims on other people, honor, love, or whatever it may be. This love cannot but give Him everything it has, without compromise. It may mean life itself, as it later meant for His dis-ciples. It may mean the treasure of this world, or happiness. No

matter. Love sees nothing but Jesus, and to love Him is all-sufficient.

Mary of Bethany lavished this kind of love on Jesus when she anointed Him, as Jesus said, for burial. And how did Jesus respond to this? The ointment was costly. One normally used only a tiny bit of it at a time, but Mary poured the whole jar upon Him at once. The disciples protested that it was an extravagance. But Jesus did not agree with them. He deemed it proper that Mary lavish the whole jar of ointment on Him. He praised what she did. He said that wherever the gospel would be preached in the whole world, what she had done would be told in memory of her (Matthew 26:10–13).

We must deeply reconsider the real meaning of the "first love," the "bridal love" to Jesus. The disciples objected to Mary's extravagant expression of love. The idea of love to Jesus which they then had is still widely held among Christians today. True enough, the disciples deemed it right that Jesus be loved and honored. But they held the same basic view which Simon the Pharisee and his guests held when the woman who was a sinner washed Jesus' feet with her tears: devotion must be moderate. They found fault with the unrestrained and unselfconscious manner in which the love expressed itself. The piously religious through the ages have always risen up in anger when they encounter such love. The Pharisees would gladly have thrown her out for her uncouth and shameless behavior—wetting Jesus' feet with her tears, then drying them with her hair. They could not recognize in this the outpouring of her love. But Jesus permitted it. He was pleased with what she had done. He saw in this deed how great her love was, and knew that it was right.

The general attitude among Christians is rather different from this attitude of Jesus. True enough, we believe in Jesus as our Saviour. But the love that suffers all, the love that spends itself

for the Beloved—this goes beyond us for the most part. When we come across such love in another person, we find it strange and hard to understand. Yet Jesus prized such love highly, when He encountered it in the house of Simon the Pharisee, and again in Bethany. He found it precious. Could it not be that He waits for such love from each one of us?

Mary wasn't the only one who gave to Jesus out of love. Scripture mentions a whole group of simple, average women who gave freely to Jesus (Luke 8:2, 3). They accompanied Him as He preached from town to town. They provided for Him out of their possessions. They turned a deaf ear to the contempt and the insults which this brought them. Their love could not do otherwise than give what they had to Jesus, and be with Him. Whatever they had of goods and property they put willingly at His disposal.

Wasn't this an extravagant use of their possessions? Weren't they responsible to their families for the way they spent their goods and property? Perhaps these things were needed at home! Perhaps they were. But this they knew: Jesus has first call upon our goods, our property, and our services. For Him, all other claims must take second place. Many voices register claim upon our energies, our money, our goods, our talents. But when Jesus claims any of these for Himself and His Kingdom, then we must listen to Him and His concerns above the claim of any others. (It is understood, of course, that this should not work severe hardship upon some other person.)

Jesus became poor for our sake (II Corinthians 8:9). This was the measure of His love. Thus He also expects from us a love that "makes itself poor." Are we ready, for the love of Jesus, to give up house, property, business, employment, loved ones? Perhaps even more difficult: are we ready to make those near us poor, by doing without us and our help? Yet those who become

poor for His sake are the recipients of His royal favor. He Himself takes care of them. For He says, "give, and it will be given to you; good measure, pressed down, shaken together, running over, . . ." (Luke 6:38). Thus our families, also, will experience the greatest blessing from Jesus when we act out of love to Him—even though our action may seem certain to hurt them. Jesus is love. Therefore He can do nothing else but give—and He gives most richly to those who lavish upon Him a love that gives freely, indeed, gives everything.

I know of a mother who loved Jesus with such an extravagant love. She gave Him that which was most precious to her: a person whom she not only loved, but on whom she depended. This woman was crippled with gout and rheumatism; often she could get about only in a wheelchair; she depended greatly upon the help of her only daughter.

Then this daughter received a clear call from Jesus to enter His service as a Sister. She knew that she could not go unless some other kind of help were found for her mother. The mother, however, thought otherwise. She loved Jesus above all else. Her heart yearned to bring Him an offering, a true sacrifice. Moved by this love, she presented Him her daughter. She told her to step out on this pathway of service for Jesus. The mother was absolutely convinced that God would take care of her, if she gave her daughter to Jesus.

The daughter entered her calling as a Sister. And God indeed helped. He gave the mother a measure of health, although it was still difficult for her to move and get around. But now her husband stepped in to help and support his wife, spending even more time in caring for her than he had previously. Out of this sacrifice of love, the love of Jesus grew to a bright flame in this woman. Many people who visited her were gripped by it.

When love for Jesus is extravagant, it is by that same token

"foolish." It must be that way. For this love is kindled by coming in contact with Jesus Christ Himself. And His love for us is indeed a "foolish love"! Therefore we also must love foolishly. It is as the Apostle Paul writes: "We are fools for Christ's sake . . . a spectacle to the world, to angels, and to men . . . we hunger and thirst, we are ill-clad and buffeted and homeless . . . we have become, and are now, as the refuse of the world, the offscouring of all things" (I Corinthians 4:10, 9, 11, 13).

The Apostle Paul could have lived quite another life. As a pious Jew, he could have lived a quiet, normal life. But love for Jesus made him a fool. He chose a life that the normal person avoids. Why? Because this love possessed him. His only thought was, "How may I please Jesus?" And so he hastened to follow Jesus along all the paths and bypaths of "foolish love." For the sake of this love, he suffered all things at the hands of other people. His patience knew no bounds. He was a doormat for other people. In the heart of the Apostle Paul burned the first love, the bridal love, which is utterly surrendered to Jesus.

St. Paul shows us that this fervent love for Jesus can grip men as fully as it can women. One finds many examples of this in the history of the Church. A whole life is set ablaze, and all human reckoning and "reasonableness" are consumed by this love which appears so foolish to the world. No wonder that Paul evoked from the governor, Festus, the response that he did. When Paul was given an audience to answer certain charges, he gave a clear theological explanation. But when he spoke of Jesus, this blazing, foolish love broke through, and Festus said, "Paul, you are mad" (Acts 26:24)!

What power lies in such a burning love! We know that purely human love, between people, can generate great

power. What then must be the unsurpassed power of this "foolish love" for Jesus? For this is a love kindled by the Creator of the heavens and the earth. In His heart is united all the glowing love in the universe. This love can undertake anything. We read, for instance, of martyrs who died on crosses, were burned at the stake, were thrown to the beasts, and yet, as the hymn writer expressed it, "they prayed for them that did the wrong." They were, as another hymn writer put it, "drunk with love." These people did not carry around in their heads a mere idea about Jesus. No, they carried *Him* in their hearts, the living One. The glow of foolish love was so mighty in them, that nothing could quench it. In their hearts echoed only one name, the name of Jesus. In the power of that name they sang songs of praise, and, like Stephen, faced wretchedness and death with joy. Love taught them to say,

> Nothing in this life hold dear,
> Nothing in the world to fear.

These were people who truly held to the first love, the bridal love. Their love bore the characteristic stamp of "foolishness." How could they react as they did, especially in the face of real suffering? Their behavior was a riddle to all who saw them. How could people be so foolish!? This love for Jesus—this foolish love—is the only explanation, for by nature we humans avoid such encounters at all costs. We use every means at our disposal to steer clear of suffering. But it is the privilege of love to go the way of suffering, for the sake of the beloved. The beloved is so dear that one yearns to show his love without stint—even if that should mean drinking the cup of suffering. The world, looking on, can make no sense out of such a sacrifice. True love for Jesus has always borne this characteristic of "foolishness." It is a sign of its genuineness, to the present day.

Is it not foolish to humble oneself before one's opponents? We remember how the love of Jesus brought a fellow worker into the kingdom of God to this point. In her service, she suffered terribly over the many ruptures in the body of Jesus. She suffered with Him, because His last prayer was taken so lightly by those who bore His name. Indeed, it was held up to scorn and ridicule. She began going to visit those who opposed her work. She wished to show them her readiness to meet them in love, and to seek with them the unity of love. This is a foolish course. It makes no sense, by the world's standards. Your opponents are sure to suspect ulterior motives.

"Here is one whom we have opposed now coming to us. She must be fishing for some favor. Or maybe things aren't going too well in her work, and she's beginning to feel guilty."

Yes, it is foolish. One must reckon to begin with that the extended hand—the offer of love—may be refused. But foolish love does it anyway out of love to Jesus. For one longs to help so that His last prayer shall be fulfilled. This love knows that it must love also one's enemies. For this was the way of Jesus, and only in this way did He win the victory.

Again, isn't it foolish to renounce and give up one's inheritance? I saw this happen in the life of a close acquaintance.

Why did she do it? Didn't she need the inheritance? On the contrary, she had her heart set on it. She had a pressing need for the money. But one of the parties named in the will made demands that were altogether unwarranted. My acquaintance didn't have any actual part in the fracas which ensued between the various parties named in the will. Nevertheless, she set aside her own claims to the inheritance. And she did it for Jesus' sake. He came that we might live together in love. He came to put an end to hate and strife. For His sake, she was prepared to give up the help which she had looked forward to receiving.

Foolish love is strong. It overcomes the instinct for self-preservation which has a deep root in all of us. In every situation, this instinct connives, so that *I* don't come out on the short end, *I* don't get too heavy a load, or *my* home or situation doesn't suffer loss. This attitude caused great difficulty in West Germany during the years when so many refugees streamed in from the East.

Yet during this time a woman in the northern portion of Hesse prepared herself inwardly to receive the refugees. Out of love for Jesus, she wanted to receive them as Jesus Himself would, according to the word of Scripture: ". . . the aliens who reside among you . . . shall be to you as native-born sons of Israel . . ." (Ezekiel 47:22).

She and her husband were both elderly, and by rights needed peace and quiet. Then, suddenly, a family of seven was referred to their house. The woman did not attempt to turn them away, nor did she utter a word of complaint. On the contrary, she received them in great love. She lived by the letter of the Scripture from Ezekiel. She divided the rooms of the house so that she and her husband received two, the other family seven. The milk from their only cow was likewise carefully divided according to the same proportion.

But it did not stop there: the last of their flour supply, the meat, the canned goods, household effects, dishes and silverware, soap and cleanser, bed linen, blankets—everything was divided in the same proportion, seven to two. The family that came as refugees was Roman Catholic. The woman of the house had never before had contact with Roman Catholics, and wondered how it would go. But God blessed this foolish love. Everything worked out perfectly. The Catholic family went to early Mass. While they were gone, the woman of the house built a fire and prepared breakfast for them in their kitchen. The Catholic

wife then prepared Sunday dinner for the Protestant couple, while they went to their services.

The elderly couple owned a small shoe factory. They had worried about what should become of it because they had no children. This concern was also taken care of. The man of the refugee family was a shoemaker. They drew up an agreement whereby he would lease the factory for a stipulated percentage of the profits.

The love between these two families was put to the test. The refugee wife took seriously ill, and for a long time the burden of caring for her and the five children fell to this elderly woman. When the refugee wife died, the lady who loved Jesus became a veritable mother to this adopted family. This foolish love bore fruit upon fruit. Their house was known in the whole town as a place of peace and blessing.

Oh! that we who receive the foolish love of Jesus might let this same foolish love grow in our own lives! It appears senseless, and yet it carries within it the greatest meaning. For it belongs to the very essence of God's own love, which embraces all wisdom. Foolish love brings with it blessing and fruit without end.

4

What Hinders the "First Love"?

Bridal love is precious beyond measure. The Enemy knows this, and therefore he begrudges it and fights against it. He seeks in every way to hinder its expression. One of his favorite techniques is to apply every possible means to *divide* our love, so that we do not give it to Jesus above all else. The Enemy knows that it is just this undivided, uncompromised love which Jesus seeks. It is His right, as Bridegroom. A bride—when she is truly a bride—gives her whole heart to the bridegroom. Her eye wanders after no other. She has heart and eye for one only. This is the kind of love that Jesus looks for in us.

We see this in the gospels. Jesus' words are clear and to the point: if we put any other love above our love for Him, then we make light of His love and His friendship. "He who loves father or mother more than me is not worthy of me" (Matthew 10:37). Jesus expects to be loved with an undivided love. Whatever else may be worthy of love pales beside the glory of His divine person. Jesus does not compete for our love. He knows that He is

beyond compare with the most desirable things that earth may offer, or that God Himself may have given—whether it be father or mother; husband, wife, child; brother, sister, or friend. Man is but a creature. Is it thinkable that our love for man should stand on the same footing as our love for Him—the Lord, and King, and Bridegroom? What are the things of this world beside Him who has created them?

This must become our thinking also. But God knows our heart. He, the great Triune God, had the same problem with His people in the Old Testament. Over and over again they put something else before Him. God spoke of it in the strongest possible terms—harlotry, infidelity, spiritual adultery! Time and again they turned from God, and refused to give Him the love for which He longed. Again and again in the Old Testament we hear the lament of the Lord:

> Your love is like a morning cloud,
> like the dew that goes early away.
> —Hosea 6:4

From a heart full of anguish we hear Him say,

> Surely, as a faithless wife leaves her husband,
> so have you been faithless to me, O house of Israel. . . .
> —Jeremiah 3:20

The people of Israel would not admit their true condition. They reasoned that they had the Temple and the worship, they prayed and read God's Word. Thus they deceived themselves into believing that everything was in order.

The prophet Jeremiah, and the other prophets, however, told a different story. They said that the people stood under the judgment of God. And why? Because they did not love God above all else. And what did the prophets mean by "love"? That which

was important to a person, that to which he gave his energy and his time, that which filled his heart, that which he desired and sought after. The love of their hearts, thus understood, was fixed on things other than God—perhaps on family or house or property; wealth, work, health, one's own honor, one's people, accumulation of worldly goods and advantages, ties to other people and nations which would bring them advantage. God would not tolerate such divided loyalties. God would not allow His people to continue to call Him their God, learn His commandments, read His Word, and pray to Him, yet all the while hold back the one thing which really counted: to love Him above all else. Therefore He set before them again and again His right to their undivided love. When they would not respond, He answered with judgment.

A divided heart was the cancer in the life of God's people in the Old Testament. It is also the cancer in the life of God's New Testament people. Our hearts have not changed or improved, no matter how we may deceive ourselves with a pasted-on piety which continually skirts the real issue of our love. Therefore in the New Testament also, Jesus must speak sobering words when He talks about our love for Him. He knows that the greatest battle in our heart takes place at just this point. No commandment is as violated as the first: to love God above all else. Jesus' words were clear and unmistakable when He said, "You cannot serve God and mammon" (Matthew 6:24). God's claim upon us is absolute. He is not content with only a part of our love. He is a jealous God. He judges nothing so severely as the service of a divided heart. We can only enter into a true love for Jesus when we sever every other tie which would bind us with a false love to a person or things.

With a view to this "first love," Jesus sets before us a bold, unvarnished question: Are you a bride or a whore? The two

possibilities are related: it is only possible to become a whore because God has called us to be a bride. The call to love God creates the alternative, that we squander our love faithlessly. Jesus looks to us for the love of a bride. Any other love which possesses our heart brings us into the state of spiritual adultery. If the thoughts and desires of our heart circle about some person, if we give him first place in our hearts, if we desire above all else to be together with him and loved by him, it is whoredom. And if it is not some person who possesses our heart, but rather some thing—my possessions, my health, my work, my favorite pastime—it is basically no different.

God demands this one thing categorically: to love Him above all other things. That says a great deal. What is the sign of a love that loves above all other things? Is it not simply this? The One whom I love is more important to me than anything else; my time is mainly taken up with Him; I do and plan everything so as to be near Him, that I might receive His love; I am ready to fulfill every wish which He makes known to me. Are God's wishes and commandments so binding upon me that I would fight and die to fulfill them? Is my heart filled with thoughts and longings for Him, or is it more taken up with other things, which come and go? Jesus knows the danger of other loves creeping into our hearts. Whenever the love for something else gains first place in our hearts, it kills our love for Jesus. Therefore He demands that we be loosed from every tie which would hinder our love for Him.

This does not mean that we are not to love people and things, indeed, everything that God has made. Jesus' concern is this: that we love all created things *in Him,* from whom and for whom they were created, and not as something independent of Him. This is the state of heart which St. Paul describes when he says, ". . . let those who have wives live as though they had

none, and those who mourn as though they were not mourning . . ." (I Corinthians 7:29, 30). In other words, our human situations and attachments are subject to Jesus. If He gives us something or someone, then we may in turn give our love to the degree and in the manner which He permits. But it also means that our heart would not be shattered if God should will that we give up some person or thing. Such an event may well shake us, but if we love Jesus above all else, we can overcome it. When our love for people and things has this character, then not only may we love them—we are commanded to do so. For God is love, and it is His will that we love. All that He has created and given must be included in our love for Him, most especially those of our own family and household, friends, and those who have blessed us in some way.

In this regard, we must recognize something about our love for other people. Since the Fall, human love is shot through with impurity and sin. Much of what passes for love is but a striving to please and satisfy ourselves. All our relationships to other people and things must come under searching scrutiny if we truly desire to enter into this "first love" with Jesus. We must submit to a thorough cleansing of our relationships. Otherwise they can become a block, and a true love for Jesus cannot break through.

This is a painful process. We avoid it all too readily. Nowhere have we constructed a more elaborate system of evasions—and all with good theological undergirding! This becomes readily apparent in practical experience. "Jesus has first claim upon our love." Christian parents believe this. They doubtless teach it to their children. But does that claim stand up when Jesus asks that they offer their child to Him? What is the usual response from parents when a daughter receives a call to His service—a call which means leaving father and mother, home and property, the

possibility of marriage and inheritance? Those of the household quickly remind her of their right to her love. And it has scriptural authority, too: "Honor your father and your mother" (Exodus 20:12). Satan still uses the same methods which he used in tempting Jesus. He tried to overcome Jesus by using the words of Scripture, but the spirit in which he used them was contrary to the spirit of Scripture. True, the Lord said, "Honor your father and your mother." But He never meant that we should do it at the price of loving Jesus less than our parents.

The subtlety of the Enemy is never greater than when he attempts to hinder our love for Jesus. What arguments and evasions he drags in as he builds his nest in our thought life! "Remember the commandment to honor father and mother . . . you have a duty to keep and manage the family house and inheritance . . . you can't let down the people who are depending on you; you are needed in your present profession . . . you owe something to your family and those you work with . . ."

But what a joy to Jesus when He finds people who stand against these blandishments—people who give room in their hearts to the undivided love which Jesus asks for.

I am reminded of a housewife and mother. She did this. Every week she gave Jesus a full half day, in which she withdrew for prayer. She asked her friends not to visit her on this afternoon of the week. To begin with, this raised more than a few eyebrows. Her family, especially, took exception to it. But she was not swayed from her purpose. Gradually the family got used to it. Indeed, as they saw what a blessing these quiet hours brought to the whole family, they were all in favor of it. They reasoned that when another person comes to see us, we set the time aside and are available. Should not Jesus also have a right to certain hours of our day?

It is a danger signal in the spiritual life when we find it diffi-

cult to say "No" to people, especially those who are dear to us. It is often a sign of a false and "soulish" bondage to that person. And whether the bonds be bold or subtle, the word of Jesus nevertheless applies:

> If any one comes to me and does not hate his own father and mother and wife and children and brothers and sisters, yes, and even his own life, he cannot be my disciple.
> —Luke 14:26

This is serious business! Whom does Jesus recognize as His disciples? Only those whose love for Him is so undivided, that for His sake they would give up even their closest blood kin.

How are we to understand this hard word of Jesus, that we are to "hate" father and mother, husband or wife and child? It is a matter of who has undisputed first place in our affections. When Jesus calls us, asking for our love, we must give it to Him without question. And if people then make demands upon us which would hinder our love to Jesus—be it parents or spouse or child—those demands must go unheeded. For when two demands are made upon me, I respond to the call and wish and will of the one whom I love the more.

This is a basic truth of spiritual life. Jesus' words declare it. Only those who love Him above all else can be His disciples. Only those who truly love Him will in turn be loved by Him. To such Jesus opens His heart.

I remember seeing this in the life of a particular individual. For a long time he had longed to experience this great love for Jesus. He sensed that something decisive was missing in his experience. Yet he could not discover the key. He applied himself to many spiritual disciplines, but without success. The hindrance was but a single thing: his heart was so full of love for

one particular person that it hindered his love for Jesus; his heart was in bondage.

At last he discovered this. This love was all-important to him. It occupied him completely. For this love he gave everything. He was prepared to fulfill the wishes of this person at any cost. For this love he would sacrifice anything. He loved this person above all else—though he had not seen it clearly, and had been convinced that Jesus had first place in his affections. When he finally saw the kind of love that Jesus actually asks of us, his heart sank within him. What was it that actually possessed his heart, in everyday life? His plans, his wishes, his activities did not center on Jesus, but on this particular person.

Through many different kinds of disappointments, Jesus broke this love to pieces. In answer to prayer, He broke the bondage of this love by the power of His blood. Only then was the way opened for this man's love for Jesus to grow. And this, alone, was the love that truly blessed him.

The way back to the "first love" is well marked. The sign reads: "Proceed only when you have set aside the hindrance of a divided heart." Many knew this love at the beginning. But then it was overgrown and choked out by so many other loves. These must be resolutely set aside, and then that "first love" will live again.

But is this really the *only* hindrance? Aren't there people whose problem and temptation is not a divided heart, and still they are not living in the "first love"?

True, there is a whole list of hindrances which keep the "first love" from breaking forth and flourishing, so that it is lost again. A second great hindrance is the effect of the Fall upon our understanding. The Enemy infiltrates our thoughts with the idea that the greatest thing, after all, is faith. ". . . . we are justified by faith . . ." (Romans 5:1). That is God's Word. It is true, and it

endures forever. Yet the same Word of God speaks over and over again about the "first and great commandment"—to love God above all else. True enough, we cannot love Jesus unless we first believe that He is our Saviour, that He has taken away our sins, that we are counted righteous before God because of Him. But we come to this faith in Jesus *in order that* we *might* love *Him.*

Faith which is a cold-blooded matter of the intellect alone is not true faith. What a caricature of faith, when it becomes a mere matter of information that Jesus lives, and that He is the Son of God who bore our sins upon the Cross. We may stand for this "faith" with resoluteness. We confess Jesus Christ when this "faith" is called into question, or even persecuted. We stand for our "faith" as a man stands—or even dies—for a conviction. Yet in all of this we are far from Jesus. Do we know how emphatically the Scripture says that those who will one day be close to Him and behold His glory are those who *love* Him (John 17:24)? We know these words by rote, and yet their inner meaning is often unfamiliar to us. For such, the day of His coming bodes darkness and disappointment: we have believed in Jesus, but we have not truly loved Him.

Only love never ends. Faith comes to an end, for then we shall see. Faith is a forerunner. It is only for our life on earth. In heaven we shall see God as He is, and faith will no longer be necessary. Here on earth, love grows in the shadow of faith. But all the while it waits with fervent longing. For it knows that it—and it alone—has appointed to it the destiny to be joined to the Beloved, to see Him face to face, and to be with Him forever.

Satan wants to rob us of this glory at all costs. He builds his nest in our minds. He assaults our thoughts. He casts shadows of suspicion upon our bridal love for Jesus. He whispers to us that this priceless love is really not worth it all. He ensnares us with catchwords and slogans. How many have held back from giving

Jesus their heart, when the epithet "Mysticism!" was hurled at them! Or "That's just a suppressed sexual drive!" No doubt it is true that some people who are emotionally sick will hug a pious feeling to themselves and call it "love for Jesus." This is just one of many kinds of manifestations of some kinds of emotional sickness. It has nothing to do with genuine bridal love for Jesus, nor should it be used to cast suspicion upon the real thing. How it must grieve our Lord Jesus to see this love for Him treated with so little feeling and understanding. This love comes to blossom in some person's heart. Almost at once he is blasted with warnings from people who know nothing of this love, and are therefore suspicious of it . . . and the love is destroyed. Would it not be better if these false guardians of our souls had millstones hung around their necks and were thrown into the sea? Jesus said that this would be preferable to causing one of these "little ones" to stumble (Matthew 18:6). And who are these "little ones"? Are they not merely those who, in the simplicity of their heart, want to love their Lord and Saviour with their whole heart, as a bride loves her bridegroom?

But again it will be said: "That's just a suppressed sexual drive. You love some person, and because there's no way for that love to express itself—say, in marriage—you give it to Jesus instead." But this overlooks or purposely ignores a plain fact of history: the fellowship of Jesus, in all ages, has included both men and women who have known the grace of the "first love," the bridal love to Jesus, and who nevertheless were married and blessed with children. No, it is not the personal love for God which is a distorted love. That is the "first," the bridal love. Distorted is the love which sets God aside, and rather than love Him above all else, loves above all else some person.

Bridal love between two people has its place, but it should not be confused with divine love. The bridal state, fatherhood,

and other such gifts which we know upon earth, are but dim likenesses and shadows of the true and real and eternal, which is above. Because there is such a thing as fatherhood in heaven, we can know something of it here on earth. All fatherhood upon earth derives its name and character from Him, the real Father. In the heavenly places there are thrones and principalities (Colossians 1:16), and therefore upon earth, fleeting and transient, are the shadows and likenesses of these heavenly realities. And because there is a Bridegroom in heaven—that is what Jesus called Himself (Matthew 9:15, 25:1)—and a Marriage Supper of the Lamb, and a Bride (Revelation 19:7), therefore upon the earth there is such a thing as a bridal state. It is but a shadow of the reality. It is a part of this present world which is passing away; for in heaven one will neither marry nor be given in marriage. Love to Jesus therefore can never be put on the same level with what we may know about human love.

Besides this objection to "bridal love," which confuses it with human love, there is another objection. It stems from some of the logical reasoning processes of our unsanctified intellect. Among Christians it is a point of contention as to precisely who is meant by the "Bride of Jesus," and who it is that receives an invitation to the Marriage Supper of the Lamb. Many Christians have arrived at the conclusion that the "Bride" consists only of Jews, while the Body of Jesus consists of believers from all nations. But if this is so, how are we to understand the fact that the Holy City, the New Jerusalem, is called "the Bride, the wife of the Lamb" (Revelation 21:1, 9, 10)? And do we not believe that through Jesus' redemption we shall be victorious, and so be privileged to live in this city? If that is so, then the inhabitants of the City of God are those who have held the bridal love for Jesus. These come from Israel, but also from other nations. As a composite group they represent a part of the "Bride of the Lamb,"

and the part is representative of the whole.

When our intellect is not dissecting the question about who is the Bride of Christ—only Jews, while the Body of Christ consists of believers from all nations—other questions will arise. The Scripture always speaks of the bride in terms of the People of Israel, or of the Church as a whole. A single individual is never referred to as the Bride of Jesus. The same basic answer applies to this question also. The Holy City is called the Bride. This simply means that all the souls in this City have lived, and are living, in this state of bridal love to the Lamb. Each individual therefore represents a bride of the Lamb.

Shall Satan's deception rob us of that which is true and real—that we are indeed called to be brides of Jesus, that one day we shall indeed sit down at the Marriage Supper of the Lamb? Satan knows well the power which lies resident in love. He knows, for the dread might of love upon the cross overcame him and hell. The needle point of his rage is directed against love. He may come garbed as an angel of light. His words will have a pious ring to them. But his objective is unmitigated: to prevent us from returning to our "first love." He knows that love wields overwhelming power. When mere obedience has utterly spent itself, love continues on. Wherever the fire of this love burns, Satan's power and position are threatened. Therefore he storms and rages whenever an individual sets his foot upon the pathway of this love. He uses any and all means to prevent us from sharing this priceless treasure.

Where an individual is living in this "first love," where "the lamp is trimmed and burning bright," Satan sets his schemes in motion: he seeks to snuff out this love in such a way that the person does not even notice that it has happened. He envies the children of men their relationship of love to their Lord and Saviour, to their Bridegroom. He knows that they are the beloved of

the Lord. He has established His kingdom and His throne for those whom He once lost. Yes, for those who love *Him*. In His kingdom they shall shine like the sun. They shall be with Him always, for they belong to Him. Satan is jealous of this love. For in love one is united with the beloved. And in the unity of love there is power. We can see this clearly when people unite together in some common cause: They are able to raise a mighty defense against their enemy. For all its timewornness, the saying is still true: "In unity there is strength." If this is true on the purely human level, consider what happens when it is raised to the divine level. Here is a human being—poor, wretched, sinful. But now, through love, he is united with Jesus Christ, the Lord and King of the whole world. Between these two is now forged a unity. And now, from this poor, wretched, and sinful human being streams forth power! Yes, a power which none can withstand! For it is a power that comes from this intimate unity with the Lord, like that of a bride with her bridegroom. And this Bridegroom has all power, in heaven and on earth!

Satan knows precisely what love to Jesus implies, for he knows who Jesus is. He knows what can happen when we give our love to Him. He knows what can issue from a union of love between Jesus and those whom He has redeemed. He knows how great and overwhelming and unsearchable it is that God should unite Himself in love with sinful human beings. He knows the almighty power of God which dislodged him from his own throne. When he looks at Jesus, he sees in Him the Victorious One, the One who smashed his own power ... with the blood of His wounds. Therefore he will risk everything, when someone unites himself in love with this Lord. Yes, Satan knows. For he has already tasted the bitter herbs of defeat at the hands of this mighty love. The ministry of one who lives in this love issues forth in the full power of the Holy Spirit. It is like a flaming

torch—that can set a whole forest ablaze. It spreads its fire to many others. For love is life, and life begets life. This is something qualitatively different than organization and preaching which is born only out of the intellect.

Satan begrudges us the power and the blessing which we find in a bridal love to Jesus. He wants to drag us into hell and outer darkness along with himself. He cannot bear to see us experience another end than the one appointed for himself. And therefore he sets himself to rob us of this love, knowing that when we lose it, we forfeit our happiness. A Christian must recognize clearly this danger from the Enemy. "Your adversary the devil prowls around like a roaring lion, seeking someone to devour" (I Peter 5:8). If he cannot succeed in altogether devouring us, he will try at the very least to devour this love. For then we are as good as dead, though still living. We are separated, both here and in eternity, from Him who is Life and Love.

Nothing is so holy, nothing so tender and delicate, nothing so easy to lose as this "first love," this bridal love to Jesus. How often Jesus uttered the warning, "Watch!" It carries the sense of "guard" or "keep." We are to be like guards or watchmen. And what is it that we are to guard and keep? More than all else we are to be on guard, to see that we remain in this "first love." We must hate and oppose anything which would hinder us from desiring and protecting this love. It cannot be that we remain strangers to this "first love." Nor can we content ourselves with saying that we knew it once, when first we found Jesus as our Saviour. No, it must be our experience today. Otherwise the warning of Jesus will come to pass with us: "I will remove your lampstand, I will snuff you out."

If the "first love" is so important to Jesus, should it not also be important to us? It is the most precious gift we can receive.

We should do battle for this love, pursue it at all costs, give everything for it. For

> If a man offered for love
> all the wealth of his house,
> it would be utterly scorned.
> > —Song of Solomon 8:7b

Yes, everything a man owns is still too meager a price for this love.

And when we do receive it, we should treasure and protect it. It is our most precious possession. We dare not lose the tiniest part of it.

5

Much Forgiveness–
Much Love

If this love to Jesus is something so precious . . .

If it is something so powerful . . .

If our lives here, and in eternity, depend upon it . . .

Then surely we could ask no more urgent and searching question than simply this: What is required, if this love is to break forth in our hearts? Further: What is necessary so that we continue to receive the gift of this love? How may it be retained? How does it grow and become strong?

God's Word supplies the answer: ". . . he who is forgiven little, loves little" (Luke 7:47). Stated positively: "He who is forgiven much, loves much." This is what Jesus said to the woman who was a sinner, in Luke 7. He said the same thing to Simon the Pharisee, in effect. He told him the parable of the creditor who had two debtors, and then posed the question: "Now which of them will love him more?" (Luke 7:42). And Simon answered: "The one, I suppose, to whom he forgave more." Jesus said to Simon: "You have judged rightly" (v. 43). In so doing, Jesus set

forth a basic spiritual truth: that person will love Jesus most who has had the greatest debt remitted, has been forgiven the most.

But didn't Simon the Pharisee also know about the forgiveness of sins? The Book of Psalms was his prayer book. He must have known by heart the words, "Blessed is he whose transgression is forgiven" (Psalm 32:1)—or the great penitential psalm, Psalm 51. Surely. But here it has to do with something more than words. It is a certain attitude of heart toward our sin, on the one hand, and the fact that our sin is forgiven and our guilt wiped out, on the other. It brings forth tears. We see them in this woman who was a sinner, who dampened Jesus' feet with her tears. She brought Him tears—tears that poured out of a broken heart. Simon knew nothing of such tears, tears of repentance. He did not cast himself at Jesus' feet, because his heart was not broken. No, he sat opposite Jesus, confident and erect. He looked down upon others, upon the woman, judging her. Nor did he stop with that. He looked down on Jesus, too. In his brazen self-confidence he called into question all that Jesus was saying and doing. This is not an uncommon attitude. We hear it expressed when God disciplines a person or a people, or when suffering comes to some person or family: we level a judgment against God, saying that this thing was not right or fair.

Simon was comfortably dressed in self-glory and self-righteousness. That was why he could not weep over his sins. He knew nothing of forgiveness, and therefore he knew nothing of this treasure on which all else depends—the love to Jesus. Jesus spoke to him earnestly: "I entered your house . . ." (v. 44)—and then follows Jesus' three-fold recital, You did not do this . . . and this . . . and this . . . but love does these things, love cannot refrain from doing them.

Here Jesus exposes to plain view the taproot of our love to Him: repentance and sorrow for our sin and guilt. When once a

person sees his guilt, and grieves over it, his heart cannot but break. He sees what he has done to other people. He cannot erase it or pay for it. His guilt crushes him to the ground, humbling him. True enough, there are people who bear a great weight of guilt, and it does not seem to bother them at all. They shrug their shoulders and say, "We're only human, after all, and we're all sinners, more or less." But such ones have never come into the situation where their hearts shudder to realize that they can neither pay for nor undo their sins.

Jesus wants to bring us into this relationship to Himself. It is the beginning point for a real love to Him. For this, one simple thing is necessary: we must recognize our sins, and this in a thoroughly practical way. We must bring to light the sins that we commit against our neighbor in everyday life—hard, judging words; envy; jealousy; faithlessness; back-biting; lovelessness; hardheartedness. With such things we bring suffering and ill upon our neighbor, and visit destruction upon his life. Yet we do not see it, and that is the great tragedy. We believe in Jesus Christ, and we admit that we sin continually against God and men. But in the practical issues of life, where guilt is real, we don't see it. On the contrary, we defend ourselves! What we did, what we said, how we behaved—it wasn't really so bad! But we are able to see quite clearly the sinful behavior in others.

This, then, is the first step. If we want to enter into a true love for Jesus, we must be prepared to have our sins dealt with. Day by day we must bring before Jesus the prayer: "Lord, give me eyes to see. Show me my sin. Show me my guilt." Day by day we must ask for ears to hear His voice when He says to us, "This . . . and this you have not given for My kingdom, this you have not done for Me, personally. You have sacrificed nothing of earthly goods for Me. Your heart clings to other people, and you have not forsaken them for my sake. And this you did not do for

Me, inasmuch as you did not do it for your neighbor, for I came to you in him."

Sin does not unsettle and grieve us until we see it clearly in a specific area of our life. The desire of God's heart is that we come to such a recognition of sin. "There will be ... joy in heaven over one sinner who repents ..." (Luke 15:7). The prayer for contrition and repentance is a prayer God will answer. And He will go further, making our sin so painful that we will fall weeping at Jesus' feet, like the woman who was a sinner. Where we have done wrong to any person, we will also humble ourselves before him, begging forgiveness.

Through repentance even sin can be turned to our profit. A woman once experienced this. For years she had a close friendship with a married man. She was a Christian. But the Enemy deceived her into thinking that God had brought her together with this man. He was the only person with whom she could discuss the questions that lay close to her heart. They understood one another as if they had been made for one another. He enriched her inner life. How could such a friendship be sinful?

But finally the light of God fell upon this relationship, and she recognized it as sinful. She saw what great guilt she bore for having destroyed the happiness of the other marriage. The word of judgment from Matthew 5 came to rest upon her conscience: even to look upon another with lust stains the heart with adultery. "If your right eye causes you to sin, pluck it out ..." (v. 29).

With that began the tears of repentance. She confessed her sin, and completely broke off her relationship with the man. And out of the grace of sorrow and repentance there grew up a great love for Jesus.

Such repentance is a joy to Jesus. And the converse, then, is also true: nothing so pained Jesus as the attitude of the Pharisees—self-righteousness and unrepentance. They knew every-

thing about God. They were conversant with God's Word. They kept the commandments, so they believed; served their neighbor, so they believed. They kept their prayer time fastidiously. Yet they knew nothing of the love of God. For one thing they could not say, with tears and pain: "God, be merciful to me, a sinner!" He who can say this from the heart is the one who loves Jesus. For he discovers that Jesus answers his repentance with forgiveness, and draws him to His heart. He discovers what the Prodigal Son discovered: despite all the sin he had piled up, the father welcomed him to the banquet table. What can one do in the face of such a love? Nothing else than respond, out of thankfulness, with all the love that one has.

What grace, that God chooses precisely *this* starting point for the renewal of the "first love": a broken heart, which grieves over its sin. This establishes the genuineness of the bridal love, for in suffering there is no deception. When my love is overlaid with sorrow, then it is genuine, for it does not proceed from mere feeling or enthusiasm. Every love for Jesus which does not root down into the soil of suffering must be viewed with some apprehension. It yields too readily to mere silliness. Like the red sky at dawning, it fades quickly away. It can even cause hurt and damage. But the broken heart of a sinner, humbled and bowed down, is something else. It does not float about in some ethereal, spiritual region. It has nothing in common with mere human enthusiasm. Further, Satan cannot tempt such a heart with high sounding phrases of love which, when unmasked, reveal a love that is altogether "soulish" and human. For Satan is haughtiness personified. He cannot humble himself. He flees from the very sight of one humble and prostrate before God. But God lifts such a one up, and takes him to His heart. His love is directed toward the sinners whom He pardons, and this love kindles their love in

return, for they can scarcely grasp it, that Jesus should love them, so laden with sin and guilt.

In all ages, those who saw themselves most clearly as sinners, those who wept over their sins, were also those who loved the most. We saw it in the Scripture in regard to Mary Magdalene. We know it also in regard to the Apostle Peter. Peter fell into sin. He denied Jesus. Then he wept bitterly over this sin. Not until this had happened did Jesus put to him the question of his love; only then could Peter answer with all his heart: ". . . you know that I love you" (John 21:15). A genuine love for Jesus had been born. And this love was protected as Peter followed Jesus into hardship and suffering, yes, even into death. To the Apostle Paul, also, was given this grace. He had persecuted the Christians. Again and again, throughout his later life, the weight of his great sin humbled him to the ground. Yet he came to love Jesus above all else, and to burn himself out in His service. Francis of Assisi was another with a great love for Jesus. The fervency of his love for Jesus still kindles that same love in people today. And it came only through deep repentance.

This is why the Lord comes into our lives again and again with severe judgments. He wants to bring us to sorrow for our sins, to a change in our ways, in order to reawaken this "first love." He must lead us along pathways of stern discipline. Moses once struck a rock until water gushed forth: God must strike our stony hearts with judgments, until tears of repentance, and streams of love break forth. He knows that in no other way will we come to this true and bridal love for Jesus. He knows us. He knows our self-righteousness, which does not need Him and His forgiveness—and therefore does not love Him. Therefore He pursues us with a love which strikes us with judgments, showing us what we are really like. He smashes our pious self assurance

and haughtiness. He brings us to ruin, and convinces us of our sinfulness.

When we recognize our sin, and our need for Jesus' forgiveness, then we ought to be drawn to Him. He is the One who has brought us to this point. And when we have tasted His forgiving love, ought we not, in thankfulness, give Him our whole heart?

The judgment blows of God bring great blessing. They lead to repentance, and then to love. I once saw this illustrated with great clarity in the life of a person whom I knew. It happened some years ago. We received news that this person had been seriously injured in an auto accident, while on a vacation trip. Her husband had been killed in the same accident. She lay in a hospital in South Germany. Theirs had been a model marriage. In one split second he had been taken from her side. She could not fathom it. Waves of despair poured over her. In her heart it was the blackest midnight. The love of her life, the one who lay closest to her heart, suddenly and unexpectedly taken from her. Inside was all emptiness and loneliness. Would this pain ever end? She could see no way out of the darkness.

She began to inquire about God once again. For long years God had not been important in her life. Now, once again, she sought contact with believing Christians. In the course of events she came to a living faith in the Lord Jesus. What an overwhelming gift thus came through this judgment blow of God. First, she came to recognize her guilt: in her former life she had closed Jesus out. Then, something new began to grow in her heart: as Jesus drew her to Himself, forgave and comforted her, a great love for Him filled her heart. Since then she has become a person of quiet serenity, who desires to follow and love Jesus.

The "first love" to Jesus is the greatest happiness, the most precious blessing which can come to us. Those who would have it must yield themselves to God's judgments. These come in a

variety of ways: through people and relationships—through everything which crosses our wishes and plans and will. Under such judgments of God, one must say: "I bow myself under Thy mighty hand, which must discipline me because of my sins." The Lord waits and yearns for our love. When He leads us along pathways of discipline, and we humble ourselves and prostrate ourselves before Him as sinners, will He not awaken this "first love" for us, and will He not renew it again and again?

Thus the way that leads us into a great love for Jesus is so simple that a child can understand and do it. We must simply learn to say "Yes" to those things which are revealed by the judgments and disciplines of God, or the reproaches of men. We must accept these judgments, and neither fight back nor excuse ourselves. When in everyday life we learn to admit our sins and mistakes, then we open the way for God to pour His love into our heart. We cannot push the blame onto others, when tensions and divisions arise between us and them. We must set aside our self-righteousness. If we fail to do this, one thing is certain: bridal love will neither grow nor remain in us. But if we honestly point out our own sins, before God and men, then God will no longer have to point them out. He will give us His love. And this love, which He pours out in our hearts, will flow back to Him as the great bridal love to Jesus.

6

Love Toward Jesus— Brotherly Love

When Jesus graces a person with His forgiving love, it quickens a single wish in his heart: to share with others the love which one has himself received. To go the way of Jesus means to live according to the pattern which He set with His own life. The characteristic mark of His life was that He totally gave Himself in love to the brethren.

Jesus' love impelled Him toward people. It compelled Him to leave the fellowship of the Father, to go forth from heaven's glory in order to share life with His creatures. Jesus is called our "Head"; we are His "members." Where He once went, He now compels us to go, for love toward Jesus makes us one with Him and His Spirit. Love toward Jesus enables us, in Him and with Him, to love all those who belong to Him—all those whom He loved and died for. Genuine love toward Jesus is more than one's own personal relationship to Him. It is more than the good feeling which a person may have. According to Scripture, it is unthinkable and impossible that a person truly loves Jesus, and

does not love the brother. To love Jesus means to serve Him in the brother. The disciples experienced this immediately after Easter. No sooner was their love newly kindled than they received their commission. Jesus questioned Peter concerning his love, and ended the conversation with the command, "Feed my lambs" (John 21:15)! Yes, when someone loves Jesus, a fervency comes upon him, and one thing he must do for Jesus: love—love as Jesus said, "By this all men will know that you are my disciples, if you have love for one another" (John 13:35). Jesus praised the woman who was a sinner, saying, ". . . she loved much" (Luke 7:47). This speaks, in the first instance, of a love for Him. But it goes beyond that, too. It also applies to relationships with one's fellow men. Francis of Assisi loved Jesus with an ardor matched by few. In Jesus he found "the Bridegroom of his soul." At the time of his conversion, as we wrote earlier, he was filled with the "sweetness of Jesus." And what was the outcome of this great love? Once Jesus had touched him, he could do nothing else than go to the leper, give him a kiss of love, and minister to his needs. When one truly loves Jesus, he can no longer live for himself. For Jesus said, "If you love me, you will keep my commandments" (John 14:15). And His commandments are compassed in a single sentence: ". . . love thy neighbour as thyself" (Matthew 22:39 KJV).

The love of Jesus sets us free from ourselves. Through the centuries it has spurred the great works of mercy in the Christian Church. According to church tradition, it was said of the early Christians, "Behold, how they love one another." What a fire of love toward Jesus burned in the breasts of Peter and Paul. Despite all persecutions, they maintained that they could not refrain from speaking in His Name. And the fervency of this love toward Jesus, in the early Christians, also embraced the brother: they shared all things in common (Acts 2:44, 45). Love toward

Jesus continually stirred His followers to new acts of love toward others. They healed the sick. They helped the poor. They cared for the widows. They fed the hungry. And this has continued down to our own day, in such things as the deaconess movement founded in Bavaria by Wilhelm Loehe. When he was asked the purpose of the movement, he wrote out this watchword: "I will serve the Lord in His wretched and His poor . . . out of thankfulness and love . . . and if I perish loving Him, He will not let me perish."

Love to Jesus flows out in love to one's neighbor. This is so natural and self-evident that the "sheep" express puzzlement when Jesus speaks to them in the Great Judgment scene of Matthew 25. "Lord, when did we see thee hungry and feed thee, or thirsty and give thee drink?" (v. 37), they ask. Jesus answers: "Truly, I say to you, as you did it to one of the least of these my brethren, you did it to me" (v. 40). In their love to Jesus they could do nothing else. They loved and served their fellow men, scarcely pausing to think about it.

To love Jesus means to share in His Nature. His love was and is a love that condescends to the poor and lowly, the despised and the insignificant. Jesus was often seen in the company of tax collectors and sinners. He lived in the companionship of simple, uneducated fishermen. He contented Himself with the goods and provisions which women supplied Him out of their belongings. Who is the object of divine love? Toward whom does it direct itself? The love which stems from our fallen human nature seeks companionship, friendship, and contact with those for whom we would have a natural liking. Our human love is attracted by the sex, or the position, or the knowledge, or the ability of the other person. We are drawn to those who suit our taste. We are on the lookout for those richly endowed with gifts and talents, whether of spirit, mind, or body. The Apostle Paul

reminds us that "God chose what is low and despised in the world . . ." (I Corinthians 1:28). Incomprehensible: the great, eternal, almighty God elects the poor and wretched among men to enter into fellowship with Himself. Therefore He looks for this same love in all those whom He, in love, has redeemed with His blood. His love is full of compassion, goodness, and forgiveness. In the faces of those who belong to Him, He looks for this same compassionate love, the reflection of His own love.

Where do we reflect the stream of this love? Where does it lead us? Are we drawn to those who, from a natural point of view, disturb us? Are we drawn to those who are quite simple in their opinions and ways and manners, who are poor in gifts of the Spirit, have little nobility of soul, and can boast nothing of birth or honor? One day we will be asked about this love, and no other: not about a love that swept us off our feet, but the love that Jesus portrayed, the love that is a reflection of God's own love. At the judgment throne of God, His own love will be the measuring stick. That will be set before us, and we will be measured against it.

God's love is by nature merciful. Its characteristic is that it can love its enemy, because it can forgive. "Love covers a multitude of sins" (I Peter 4:8) and keeps no account of wrongs. Therefore when a person holds out for his rights against another, even to the extent of taking the issue to court, it is no longer a reflection of Jesus and His forgiving love. Rather, it is a reflection of hell. For Satan is the accuser, who keeps account of everything against us. But when we belong to Jesus, when His love grips us, then Satan has no more power. He cannot drive a wedge between us and our brother.

What further characterizes the love of Jesus, and therefore also the love of those who live in true bridal love with Jesus? Jesus loves all people. He is one with the Father, who "so loved

the *world"* (John 3:16). Those who are in Christ cannot love only the brethren who are close to them, nor only a part of mankind. They must love all men, friend and foe alike. One who loves Jesus must have a large heart. His love must embrace everyone. He builds no fences. His love is not limited to his own community, to his own human or spiritual family, his own church or fellowship group, his own state or nation. He sets no such limits. For this love of Jesus never ceases. It may be forsaken. It may be treated like an enemy. It may encounter ingratitude and evil. Yet it persists, even though it must forgive "seventy times seven" (Matthew 18:22).

This lowly, forgiving, merciful, and all-embracing love is not easily obtained. By ourselves it is altogether impossible to attain. This is one of the most difficult aspects of our lives. Again and again we stumble and fall at just this point: we cannot forgive, cannot be merciful; with difficult people our love simply falls short of the mark. We excuse our failures by saying that it is impossible. But do we consider what that implies? It implies that it is impossible to have the right kind of love toward Jesus.

What a joy to know that the requirement for true bridal love toward Jesus is not anything we do. Rather, it is a broken heart, which is convicted of its failures and sins. And a true love for one's brother is born along this same pathway. One sees that he has nothing of real love in himself. He sees all his guilt, his lovelessness. Again and again this drives him to Jesus, who alone is the wellspring of love. Out of His heart of love, Jesus gives a true love for one's brother. As Jesus gives us this love, we learn more and more to love His creatures. We stop putting limitations and fences around our love. More and more we are given to love all that He has created, the entire universe. St. Francis is once again a marvelous example of this. All God's creatures were enfolded in his love. He preached to the birds. He lifted a worm from the

pathway. And not only that: he spoke of "brother wind" and "sister sun."

Jesus' love was not exhausted with a few friendly words and affectionate feelings. His love proved itself in that He humbled Himself and became a servant to all. He emptied Himself of all honor, wealth, and privilege. He was obedient even unto death. These same characteristics will mark the life of His disciples, who are filled with His love. They seek no other right than the right to sow love. They submit themselves to the other person. They are able to make any sacrifice, to give up everything. They seek not to rule, but to serve. Such a love toward Jesus has a special characteristic: it is prepared to die. Yet it, alone, has life. Jesus' love for us brought Him to His death. Yet that love now kindles in us the true bridal love. When the flame of that love burns within us, it makes us ready to die for the brethren. We can say with the Apostle Paul, "Therefore I endure everything for the sake of the elect, that they also may obtain salvation in Christ Jesus with its eternal glory" (II Timothy 2:10). Yes, giving everything—if only some might be saved.

When one loves Jesus, he is zealous to save all those whom Jesus loves. This is the impulse behind missionaries, who proclaim the glory of His name. This is what impelled the apostles to go to strange lands and cities. They could not keep silent concerning this name, in which they had found salvation and blessedness. This was the message they carried to both Jews and heathen. Bridal love to Jesus brings with it a fervency to make known who the Beloved is, who has captured our hearts. One must praise His beauty, His love, and His power to redeem. One burns with a love for the brethren, that they also might have a share in this most precious blessing, the love of Jesus.

Those who have had a great love for Jesus have had tongues like a well sharpened pencil. Their words have gone like arrows

into the heart, kindling a love for Him who is their salvation and blessedness. All true missionaries have been ambassadors of His love. They themselves have first been enthralled with this love. Like the two disciples on the road to Emmaus, they have said, "Did not our hearts burn within us while he talked to us . . . ?" (Luke 24:32). Full of joy and the Holy Spirit, they have then witnessed of this Jesus who has inflamed their heart. From this love streams forth a love to all His children—but especially to those who are far off, and who most seek His love.

What a wonderful might lies in this great love of Jesus! It enables us to become a blessing to our brothers. It makes us witnesses who can make known His love with spiritual power. In saving and redeeming us, He gives us a message for others—that they, too, might know Jesus, might give their lives for the brethren, and follow Jesus in all things.

7

Love Toward Jesus—
the Fellowship of
His Sufferings

Those who love want to spend all their time with the one whom their souls love. So also, those who love Jesus want to be near Him. They go where He goes. And Jesus, on His part, returns that love; He wants those who love Him to be with Him. That is what He means when He says ". . . where I am, there shall my servant be also . . ." (John 12:26). In heaven those who love Jesus will share His life there—a life of glory, royal power, and heavenly blessedness. But if our love is genuine, we will also be ready to share His life upon earth, so long as we are here.

Again and again Jesus has called those who belong to Him to follow Him along His earthly pathway. "If I then, your Lord and Teacher, have washed your feet, you also ought to wash one another's feet" (John 13:14). ". . . Whoever would be great among you must be your servant, . . . even as the Son of man came not to be served but to serve . . ." (Matthew 20:26, 28).

With such words He summons us to go with Him along the pathway of humility and lowliness. And He says further: "it is enough for the disciple to be like his teacher, and the servant like his master. If they have called the master of the house Beelzebul, how much more will they malign those of his household" (Matthew 10:25). "Remember the word that I said to you, 'A servant is not greater than his master.' If they persecuted me, they will persecute you . . ." (John 15:20). "The cup that I drink you will drink; and with the baptism with which I am baptized, you will be baptized" (Mark 10:39).

Here upon earth, those who go with Jesus go with Him in His sufferings. Here upon earth Jesus carried His cross. Nor was it a one-time event. Cross-bearing marked His whole life. Thus He says to His disciples: ". . . take up [your] cross and follow me" (Matthew 16:24). Indeed, He says, "Whoever does not bear his own cross and come after me, cannot be my disciple" (Luke 14:27). This is how a disciple proves his love for Jesus. He chooses unconditionally to be with Jesus, to accompany Him on His way, to follow Him at all costs. This is not a mere act of remembrance. Love for Jesus does not merely identify with those sufferings which He endured while here upon earth. It also shares in those things which He suffers today, as the living and ever-present Christ.

When a bride loves her bridegroom, she goes the way that he goes, even though it may be hard. She does not ask whether the way will be hard, nor what difficulties may lie ahead. Only one thing counts: that she be with her bridegroom, that she share in his life. Love compels us to share precisely those hard things which the beloved must bear. It is a privilege to be drawn into this inner sanctuary of the beloved's need. It is a great gift to be trusted. Those who have experienced this know how precious it is.

Love knows only one grief: to be separated from the beloved. This is the greatest pain one must suffer. If, in sharing the life of the beloved, one experiences some pain or despair, that is small in comparison with the pain of being separated from the beloved. Love, which sees the beloved suffering, at once seeks a way to help bear this suffering. We see this theme expressed in the opera *Fidelio:* the husband is in prison, and the wife cannot rest until she herself finds a way to get into the prison. If this is true of human love, how much more is it true when the love of loves, the love of Jesus, takes possession of us?

The disciple, who loves Jesus, sees Him as an infant. His bed is a hard, bare manger in a stable. Then he sees Him as a man, dying upon the cross. How poor and naked and helpless and obscure is his Lord! All at once he feels uncomfortable in his station as a Christian. He needs the "mind of Christ," which St. Paul tells us about in his letter to the Philippians. Jesus became poor for us. Therefore his disciple must give away earthly goods, and experience something of poverty, in order to come truly close to Jesus.

The disciple knows that Jesus is the King of Glory, the Creator of the world and of men. Yet he must watch Him grow up as an unknown carpenter's son, must see Him walk the earth as a traveling preacher, without reputation, without honor, continually humiliated by the Pharisees. Seeing this, the true disciple longs to come close to Jesus, and go with Him along this hard pathway. In his profession or his circle, the disciple seeks a place without honor, or recognition, or influence. Rather, he seeks to live in such a way that he will remain poor, unknown, and without reputation.

"First love" seeks in concrete ways to go with Jesus along the way of poverty and lowliness. When this love lays hold upon a person, it can bring him to give up everything, even though he

is much caught up in life and high up in his profession.

A teacher once received a call from Jesus to go the way of poverty and lowliness. He asked her to come with Him, and serve the poorest of the poor. She was highly respected in her profession for her capability. She had excellent retirement benefits. Her health was not good, and therefore the hospitalization and retirement benefits in her present profession meant a lot to her. Yet she loved Jesus, and knew that He was waiting for her to go this other way.

She chose His way. She resigned her position, thus giving up her medical and retirement benefits. She entered the Sisterhood, in which she had no medical or retirement insurance. She worked in a kindergarten in a housing development. The children were very poor, and the work often hard. For this service of love to "the poorest of the poor," she received no compensation: together with the other Sisters, she had to look to the Lord in faith for everything that she needed. Yet she went this way joyfully, in love to Jesus, and became a blessing to many.

Jesus' way was not only a way of poverty and lowliness. It became at the end the way of suffering. The disciple must look upon this One whom he loves, see Him crowned with thorns, with a mock scepter in His hand, spit upon, mocked, reviled. And the true disciple still wants to be with Jesus, even here. Love compels us to go willingly with Jesus through suffering. Men may cut us off, may blacken our reputation and slander our name, because we go this way of Jesus without compromise. But that is our way.

The one who loves Jesus sees Him carry His cross toward Golgotha. Again and again He breaks down under its weight. Only one helped Jesus on His way to the cross, Simon of Cyrene, and he was forced into it. Today Jesus still bears the cross of the world. He must pick up and carry all the crosses which His dis-

ciples have cast aside. The true disciple sees this. His love for Jesus quickens in him a burning desire to stand with Jesus in this also. "Lay it on me," he says. "I will carry it gladly." He bows down under the load that God lays on him, and day by day gives thanks that also here he can be with the One whom he loves. He knows how closely united he is with his Lord, when he goes this way of the cross.

Yet this love, which wants to go with Him on His way of suffering—how often Jesus has been denied it by His disciples—then, and now! True enough, His disciples were with Him during the years of His traveling ministry. Out of love for Him they had given up everything. They shared hardship and poverty with Him. Yet their love was still small. It was not yet the real bridal love. Their desire to share all things with Him had a limit. They were not prepared to go into suffering with Him. Before His passion began, Jesus had said, "Where I am, there shall my servant be also." But who among His disciples did He find, when He entered into His sufferings? In dark Gethsemane they left Him alone and slept. When He was taken captive they fled. When He was taken bound to Caiaphas, not one of His disciples could be found who would openly identify with Him. The lone disciple who observed the trial, standing at some distance in the court-yard, denied Him. In all five of the hearings which He under-went, Jesus stood before His judges alone. Nor was any disciple at His side when they scourged Him, when they crowned Him with thorns, when He went out bearing His cross. At the Cross itself stood but a single disciple, John.

Perhaps that word came back to them later: "Where I am, there shall my servant be also." Perhaps the accusation of that word went like a needle into their hearts: we were not with You, when it came right down to it! And perhaps this word became a guide in days to come. When repentance had brought forth true

love in them, this word would be a constant reminder to be found in that place where the Lord was, cost what it may. And this they did. They went with Jesus the way of the cross—into suffering, persecution, and death. And therefore, in heaven above, they will once again be with the Lord whom they loved with all their hearts—be with Him in His glory.

Today Jesus seeks those who will love Him. Those who will not desert Him, as His disciples did when He entered into His passion. Rather, those who will stay with Him as the disciples did after His resurrection. Those who, today, will become disciples of the cross, out of love for Him.

Only those who love Him will long for such a life of discipleship. They want to be with Him at all times, in every situation. Of itself, their life may be a happy one. Yet they can no longer live alone, separated from Jesus. He has become their life. Those who love Him have learned that where the Lord Jesus is, there is life. He is the wellspring of joy and happiness, even in the midst of sorrow. He Himself is joy and peace and contentment.

Those who go the way of the cross with Jesus are drawn into one of the great secrets of the heart of God: the pearl of great price, the hidden treasure, is found at the bottom of the cup of suffering. In suffering, the true and deepest love will be put to the test, for it will receive the key to God's own heart and love. The Spirit of God will reveal what lies upon His heart, His love, and His suffering. He suffers for all those who are His children, yet have not come home to His heart. He cherishes a love for all His human children. He gave Jesus up to death for them. Yet He is but little loved in return, not even by His own, and in this He suffers. He suffers over His beloved chosen people, Israel, for they still have not come home to Him through the sacrifice of His only begotten Son. He suffers over all the divisions between the members of the Body of Jesus. He suffers whenever the pow-

ers of sin and darkness prevail over His human children.

Those who love God will find that His pain becomes their own pain. As disciples of Jesus they are privileged to share the suffering, the concern, the burden of their Master. As children of God they share the pain of the Father. They see the One whom they love suffering. They want to help carry that burden of suffering, take it upon themselves where possible. And thus, out of love, they can say with the Apostle Paul: "I rejoice in my sufferings . . ." (Colossians 1:24). Why did Paul break into joy at the thought of his sufferings? How can a person rejoice over suffering? He rejoiced because he was privileged to go the way of Jesus. The signposts along that road read Poverty, Lowliness, Enemies, Slander, Persecution. Yet in the midst of all that he can rejoice, because he suffers it for Jesus' sake. That is why he can even praise the value of suffering, in Romans 5:3. And he knows that in suffering he is able to comfort and help His Lord in one of His greatest sorrows—His sorrow over His imperfect and incomplete Church. Indeed, through suffering he will help to perfect and complete it. ". . . in my flesh I complete what is lacking in Christ's afflictions for the sake of his body, that is, the church" (Colossians 1:24).

What a privilege Jesus has given His disciples! A privilege reserved for those who love Him. What overwhelming trust, that He thus opens to us His innermost heart! His chosen Bride will not come to perfection and blessedness and glory except through tribulation. And He permits His disciples, through their sufferings, to fulfill what is lacking in the Bride's tribulation. Could there be any greater privilege than to be taken into this "fellowship of his sufferings" (Philippians 3:10 KJV)? Should not a disciple, who loves Jesus avail himself of this privilege? Should it not be the most sacred offer which could come to him, a treasure which he guards with all care, which he would not give up

for anything? Few people have found this precious treasure, though the Scripture speaks clearly of it under various figures. But those who love Jesus will desire this treasure fervently. For true love always summons us to sacrifice, to a sharing of the cares and sufferings of the beloved.

Yet a delicate veil always lies over everything that has to do with love to Jesus, or the sacrifice which springs from this love. The love between God and man is enfolded in mystery. In Ephesians Paul writes about this intimate union, dimly shadowed in the marriage relationship: "This mystery is a profound one, and I am saying that it refers to Christ and the church" (Ephesians 5:32). Scripture also speaks about the mystery of the rapture (I Corinthians 15:51). Here, too, the central issue is love, for only those who love Jesus will be raptured, and be with Him always.

Only in a few places does the Scripture shed light on these things. The Apostle Paul writes that he was caught up into the third heaven (II Corinthians 12:2). Several times he says that he has entered into suffering for the sake of other souls (II Corinthians 12:15, Philippians 2:17, Colossians 1:24, II Timothy 2:10). In one place he says that he bears the marks of Jesus' wounds (Galatians 6:17). He was utterly united with the sufferings of Jesus. God perhaps laid upon him the visible marks of all his suffering in soul and spirit and body. As a servant he was truly in the place where his Master was. He was always with Jesus upon this way of suffering, and bears witness to it continually (I Corinthians 4:17).

But who today knows anything about this fellowship of love—this fellowship of suffering—with Jesus? Who knows anything about suffering for God's chosen ones, in order that they may inherit eternal blessedness? Who knows anything about suffering for His Church, that she be made perfect? Yes, who suffers the pain of all the imperfection and division in God's Church?

Who is it that can truly rejoice when through his suffering here something can be done to build her up? We have not yet been put to the great test of suffering. But who among us makes use of the many everyday opportunities which do present themselves?

In the first centuries the spirit that summoned people into suffering still lived in many of Jesus' disciples. The "first love" still burned brightly. It was a power which compelled them to sacrifice for Jesus, and therefore also for His Church, His chosen ones. These ones who loved Him, and who proved their love by suffering, became the seed of the Church of Jesus Christ. And such ones have been found down through the history of the Church. In fervent love they have gone this way with Jesus. In the fellowship of His sufferings they have become blessing-bearers for the Church.

We see such examples in some of the Christian martyrs at the time of the Russian revolution. In more recent times, a man like Pastor Paul Schneider witnessed to such a love with his life and his death. He died painfully in the Buchenwald concentration camp because he dared to stand for the truth of God's Word against the leaders of the Third Reich. He never swerved in the least from this pathway of suffering, nor did he seek to ease his own lot where he might have. He underwent the torture of the death cells as if it were nothing, if only he might call out the good news of the gospel to his fellow prisoners. Love comes the closest to God in suffering. Something of his experience of this comes out in words from his diary: "The darkest hours of our life bring us the closest to God, for which we owe Him the greatest thanks."

Today the Lord waits for such faithful love, such willingness to suffer—and especially so among us, for we are entering into the end times.

8

Jesus' Second Coming– a Time of Separation

The end of all things is at hand" (I Peter 4:7). Our generation can say this in a way that earlier generations could not. The signs of the times, which herald the coming of the end, are fulfilling themselves before our eyes. Jesus said that we should take heed of these signs. From all nations, Israel is returning to the land of its fathers. This was prophesied as a sign of the end (Ezekiel 38:8, 39:28). The Gospel is carried to the most distant and remote corners of the earth (Matthew 24:14). And now we have entered into the Atomic Age. The devastation portrayed by the trumpets of judgment is at our threshold (Revelation 8 and 9).

Yes, we are on the threshold of the Second Coming of Jesus, as it is written:

> For the Lord himself will descend from heaven with a cry of command, with the archangel's call, and with the sound of the trumpet of God. And the dead in Christ will rise first; then we who are alive, who are left, shall be

caught up together with them in the clouds to meet the
Lord in the air; and so we shall always be with the Lord.
—I Thessalonians 4:16, 17

But who will have a part in thus retracing the pathway of His
Ascension? Who belongs to this company of His which will be
raptured to Him: when the cry of command resounds, and the
voice cries out: "The Bridegroom cometh"? Only those who hear
the voice. And this will not include all who call themselves by
His name. Why? Because we only hear the voice of one whom
we truly know and love—especially when many voices surround
us. Love picks out the voice of the beloved, and is able to follow.

On that day Jesus' voice will sound forth like the roar of
mighty waters, like a cry on a battlefield. But the voices of this
world are also loud in these days. And they will make still more
noise as we move into the end times. Who will be able to hear
Jesus' voice in such a din? Only those who love Him. The others
will not perceive it.

It was the same during Jesus' days upon the earth. Many saw
Him, yet did not recognize Him. They heard Him, but did not
receive His words. "But to all who received Him, who believed
in his name, he gave power to become children of God" (John
1:12). These He will receive into His heavenly Kingdom, and
they will be with Him forever. For children of God must be with
their Father; and members of Jesus must be with their Head.
Jesus will Himself come and get those who belong to Him. He
will come in the clouds of heaven and receive them unto Himself.

Those who love Jesus long to be with Him—always and forever. Separation always brings sorrow to those who love. Jesus'
love will answer this longing. The Marriage Supper of the Lamb
draws nigh. The nearer we come to the day of His Second

Coming, the harder it will be for Jesus' love to wait. And in these last days of tribulation, those who belong to Him will yearn for Him with deepest longing. For does not love seek union with the beloved especially in times of distress? At such times they want the beloved to be as close as possible.

We see this in human relationships. A bride and a bridegroom can get lost in a crowd of people so that one scarcely notices that they belong together. But let fire break out, or some danger arise, and one soon sees who belongs together as bride and bridegroom. They stand to the danger as one, not arbitrarily, but because they are bound together by the law of love. It will be like that in the last times. Those who are bound together by divine love will find each other. The separation will be made, for the last time is a time of separation. It is the time of the great judgment. But judgment begins in the household of God (I Peter 4:17). It separates those who do not belong in the kingdom of God.

Upon earth the night will become darker. Wars and rumors of war will increase. Unrighteousness will prevail. The "mystery of iniquity" will bestir itself. The son of perdition, who opposes all godliness, will be slowly revealed, and begin to exercise his power and influence (II Thessalonians 2:3ff KJV).

He casts a spell even over believers, in whom love has grown cold. They have fallen under the power of wars and strife, unrighteousness, and the lying wonders of Satan (Matthew 24). He will draw them like a magnet—all those whose hearts belong to him, because they are of like nature. But Jesus will draw all those betrothed to Him, who love Him and reflect His nature. There will come a separation between those who have been together for a long time. Perhaps they have been members of the same congregation or fellowship. They both seemed to be living in preparedness for the Lord's Coming. But in that day two will

be together in the field; Jesus will take one, catching him away, but the other will be left (Luke 17:36 KJV). Every single individual—whether he wants to or not, whether he knows it or not—will be drawn to one pole or the other, either to Christ or to the Antichrist.

What a horrible realization: believing Christians, unknowingly and imperceptibly, come under the influence of the Antichrist. And why does the Prince of Darkness prevail against them? Because they have not taken care that the flame of love was burning brightly in them. Therefore much darkness and impurity could remain in them. And one day they wake up to find themselves standing in the ranks of the Antichrist. They were not vigilant while there was still time to cleanse out the old leaven. They have sown lukewarmness and conformity to the world. Now they will reap: the Prince of this World swallows them up, as he sets up his kingdom.

In this time immediately preceding the time of the Antichrist, our devotion to Jesus must be complete. Our love toward Him must be extravagant, foolish, ready to sacrifice. We can no longer afford a half-hearted battle against sin. The end times are times of crisis and judgment. It is a time of either-or: either we are taken away by Jesus, or we are left behind under the reign of the Antichrist. For in those days will be revealed the head of the Kingdom of Light, and the head of the Kingdom of Darkness: Jesus will come on the clouds of heaven, and Satan will appear upon earth as man. Each gathers his host, in preparation for the final conflict And then they will draw up for battle: Jesus with His chosen ones—the Antichrist with his followers.

Then it will be revealed to which head the members belong. Every veil will be torn away. Every appearance will be exposed. The true nature of every man will be revealed. Then will be seen what every soul has really been living for. The true master of

every heart will be brought to light. It will not matter what denomination or group one has belonged to. Now the only question is: To whom does our heart belong, whom have we loved above all else? ". . . at his coming those who belong to Christ . . . shall all be made alive" (I Corinthians 15:23, 22). And, ". . . we who are alive, who are left, shall be caught up together with them in the clouds to meet the Lord in the air" (I Thessalonians 4:17).

The Lord said that there are those who are dressed in sheep's clothing, but inwardly are ravenous wolves: unforgiving, rebellious, full of the mob spirit, venomous, slanderous, jealous. How many such will be exposed in that hour? The Scripture says that such will not inherit the kingdom of God (Galatians 5:19–21). In that moment when Jesus comes to fetch His own, the doorway to heaven will close for those who have led lives of deception. Those who have the "name of being alive, and . . . are dead" (Revelation 3:1), will be left behind. It is not only those who cherish evil in their hearts who do not inherit the kingdom of God. Jesus speaks a similar word about dead, lukewarm members of the Body of Christ: ". . . I will spew you out of my mouth" (Revelation 3:16). Why? Because spiritual death is a sign of a dead love. Where life is, there is love. According to Scripture, Life and Love are alike expressions of God's nature: God is Life, and God is Love. And therefore they must remain behind. They did not love Jesus. They did not prepare themselves for the Marriage Supper, as a true bride.

Then will rise up the great lament and mourning of those left behind. The despairing cry will come from the lips of many who knew Jesus: "Too late! Too late! The door is closed! The door is closed!" Many thought that their place at the Marriage Supper was assured. But in that hour Jesus speaks to them the hard words: "I do not know you" (Matthew 25:12). He recognizes as

His disciples, as His Bride, only those who have loved Him, and out of love followed in His footsteps. These do not have the name of being alive only. They bear life in themselves. The fire of love burns in their hearts. That is why the Bridegroom recognizes them as His own. For He Himself is eternal love. He bears in His heart the fire of a love which one day will fill the whole world. The Second Coming of Jesus is thus the coming of Love; the coming of the Bridegroom to those who love Him. Only those will be taken in to the Marriage Supper of the Lamb.

When faith looks toward the Second Coming of Jesus, it sees love as the principal issue. This is the one question that will be asked when we stand before the Lord. The same question He asked Simon Peter: "Do you love me?" In that hour the truth of Jesus' word will be realized: that He will reveal Himself to those who love Him; that those who "have loved his appearing" (II Timothy 4:8b) will receive a crown at the Marriage Supper. "She has loved much," Jesus once said. On the day of His Coming, such praise will be precious, more precious than all the goods and treasures of this world. For only those who love Him, those who bear the insignia of the Bride, will experience the grace of union with Him. They alone will be raptured. No other souls will behold Him when He comes on the clouds of Heaven. In that hour He reveals Himself as the Bridegroom to the Bride who loves Him. His Coming at this time is special and unique. Not everyone will see His beauty, glory, and majesty. Only those who are invited to the Marriage Supper of the Lamb. Only those of whom it is said,

> and his Bride has made herself ready;
> it was granted her to be clothed with fine linen, bright and pure.
> —Revelation 19:7, 8

These are the ones who have a fervent love for Jesus. For the true adorning of a bride is her love.

This is the hour of preparation. Therefore the Scripture speaks to us and says, "work out your own salvation with fear and trembling" (Philippians 2:12), for without holiness "no one will see the Lord" (Hebrews 12:14). Without holiness, no one can go to meet Him, no one can behold His countenance. Only the pure in heart can see Him (Matthew 5:8). The Scripture goes on to say, "And every one who thus hopes . . . [the hope of seeing Him] purifies himself as he is pure" (I John 3:3). The Scripture holds out to us such a bold hope, that on the day of rapture, the day of the Marriage Supper, we may be sanctified, and transfigured into His image. Love is the only motive which constrains us to be purified and cleansed. A bride does everything to accommodate herself to the bridegroom, and please him, because she loves him. Should not a bride of God be the first to do it?

A true bride enters into a battle of faith against sin. A fight to the finish. She takes the call of her Bridegroom seriously, and seeks to follow it: "Repent, for the kingdom of heaven [the Coming of the Bridegroom] is at hand" (Matthew 3:2). Out of love for Him, she will be prepared for Him—at any cost. She pursues this goal zealously, as the Apostle Paul did for those who were entrusted to him: "I feel a divine jealousy for you, for I betrothed you to Christ to present you as a pure bride to her one husband" (II Corinthians 11:2). The bride lives for this hope. She is going to see Him! She is going into the Marriage Supper with Him! She can tolerant no disfigurement in herself; love would not allow it. She wants to delight the eyes of her Bridegroom, who will "present the church to himself in splendor, without spot or wrinkle or any such thing, that she might be holy and without blemish" (Ephesians 5:27). The entire

adorning of the bride has but one objective: to one day hear Him speak the words,

> You are all fair, my love;
> there is no flaw in you.
>   —Song of Solomon 4:7

She knows that she pleases the Bridegroom best when garbed in humility. In His Word, the Lord has said that He is pleased to dwell in humble hearts. Therefore she submits to all disciplines which will conform her to the image of Jesus. She knows that we must be disciplined in order to partake of His holiness.

So love sets itself to attain to this final goal—union with the Lord, the rapture, the first resurrection, beholding the face of the Holy One Himself, the very Son of God. Yet who can endure the Coming of the Lord? Jesus' eyes are like flames of fire (Revelation 1:14). The light that streams from His countenance is overwhelming. No iniquity can endure that light. No soul bound in darkness can face it; in terror they cry out, to the mountains and rocks, "Fall on us and hide us from the face of him who is seated on the throne, and from the wrath of the Lamb" (Revelation 6:16). To encounter Jesus thus is to face the greatest hour of decision. Those who are conformed to His image will be united with Him. Those who do not bear His image will be hurled away from the presence of His countenance. That is why Jesus spoke so urgently when He thought about the hour of His Coming: "But watch at all times, praying that you may have strength to escape all these things that will take place, and to stand before the Son of man" (Luke 21:36).

The door to Heaven and to the Marriage Supper will be open to those who love, those who are awake and prepared. Love is the key. Do we have this key now in these last days, when the Coming of Jesus is upon the very threshold? We do not know the

day or the hour. But we know that it is close at hand. The watchmen on the battlements of the City of God are blowing their trumpets. The cry resounds: "Make yourself ready, the Bridegroom comes, the King." Who can go out to meet Him? Who can behold His face? Who will abide with Him forever? The souls that love. Love seeks Him fervently, even knowing that His holiness could consume it utterly. And yet divine love cannot cast away the one who comes in love. And so Jesus will open the door to this Bride who comes in love. She will go in, and celebrate the Marriage with Him.

9

The Final Goal of Love—
the Marriage Supper
of the Lamb

God's word says, "Blessed are those who are invited to the marriage supper of the Lamb" (Revelation 19:9). Blessed indeed are they. What will that day bring? What will it mean to come into the Marriage Supper? It is beyond the power of thoughts or words to express. All the joy and bliss of this earth cannot be compared with the Marriage Supper of the Lamb. It is the great festival of love. The King of heaven and all worlds gives a feast, His own bridal feast, with the Bride of His love. It is a royal and heavenly feast, worthy of the One who has prepared it, sparing nothing.

How the angels who serve Him hasten to prepare the Marriage Supper! Myriads of angels—ten thousand times ten thousand! How the "ministering spirits [who are] sent forth to serve, for the sake of those who are to obtain salvation" (Hebrews 1:14) scurry about! The table for the Marriage Supper must be

prepared and decked in heavenly beauty. If the angels have served the faithful here upon earth, how much more shall they serve them above. When they come into the Father's Kingdom as kings, they shall serve them without end! The choirs of seraphim and cherubim will sing their loveliest songs. They will praise Jesus for the Bride who sits at His side, lovely beyond compare. For the blood of the Lamb has transformed sinners into His Bride. They bear His image. They sit with Him upon His throne (Revelation 1:5, 6; 3:21; Ephesians 5:25–27). Unnumbered choirs of angels will swirl in dance around the King and His Bride at the Marriage Supper of the Lamb. All heaven will break out in song and shouts of joy; the harp will be heard; the sounds of praise will never die away. The Bride will be taken into this festal celebration of all heaven . . . will enter into the splendor and beauty of the Marriage Supper hall, where lights not of this earth stream forth in heavenly magnificence.

Yet in the midst of all this glory, the Bride will be as one in a dream. As one who truly loves, she has eyes only for one, for Him whom her soul loves, the Lamb in the midst of the throne, her Bridegroom. Amidst all the jubilation of angel voices, she listens for but one voice, the voice of the King of kings. For now she may remain with Him forever and ever. She may see Him face to face. For now His unveiled glory has been revealed, and it overshadows all the splendor of heaven and cherubim. Ten thousand times ten thousand angels may radiate their splendor in heaven. Even one angel can brighten the earth with his splendor (Revelation 18:1). Yet this light is as nothing when He appears. He fills all heaven with His splendor, shines more brightly than many suns: Jesus! Therefore it is written, "And the city has no need of sun or moon to shine

upon it, for the glory of God is its light, and its lamp is the Lamb" (Revelation 21:23).

Indeed, light and glory flood forth from the face of Jesus. It spreads through all of heaven, immersing everything in splendor and beauty. Everything there is but a reflection of this One, Jesus—angels, the redeemed, the glow and splendor of the golden city itself. Yes, Jesus. Jesus, whose love and unspeakable beauty lends its glory to everything that lives in heaven. It could not be otherwise. Everything radiates a wondrous splendor, for everything lives in direct contact with Him, under His dominion. Here nothing can stem His influence. Upon earth He had to break through many layers of sin and the power of the enemy. But here the power of Jesus' love can radiate everywhere and have its full effect. That is why heaven is so heavenly bright. The golden streets, the walls of jasper, the crystal stream—all are clear and transparent. In the City of God, everything is like a "booster station" for love. Every tree and every leaf has been individually created to receive the splendor and beauty of Jesus, reflecting and passing it on in a variety of ways. It is truly a "City of Jesus," this New Jerusalem. Every soul lives in the presence of His splendor.

The Bride will see the King in His beauty. She will speak to Him, though surely in a different way than she did upon earth.

> You are the fairest of the sons of men;
> grace is poured upon your lips.
> —Psalm 45:2

There will be intimate conversation, such as we see foreshadowed in the Song of Solomon, where the bridegroom speaks to his bride in great love and happiness: "How sweet is your love, my sister, my bride!" (Song of Solomon 4:10a). And the bride calls out:

My beloved is all radiant and ruddy,
distinguished among ten thousand.

This is my beloved and
    this is my friend,
O daughters of Jerusalem.
        —Song of Solomon 5:10, 16

Yes, there will be an ardent conversation between Bride and
Bridegroom, for love answers to love, and proves itself in words
and deeds.

And at the glance of the majestic, kingly, divine Bridegroom,
her Lord, the Bride can only sink at His feet and adore Him. But
He raises her up and seats her at His right side. For she is His
Bride. She is the one of whom it is written, "at your right hand
stands the queen in gold of Ophir" (Psalm 45:9b). In the fires of
tribulation her faith and love have proved themselves. Now she
radiates a heavenly splendor and beauty. Who could ever recognize the old sinner, in such a Bride. She is robed like a queen,
in white linen, crowned with the crown of righteousness (II Timothy 4:8). And so she sits at the side of the King of all Kings, and
celebrates marriage with Him.

Now she wears the crown whose glory is the counterpart of
the humiliation and shame which she bore for the sake of His
Name, in patience, humility, and love. She is the Bride of the
King of the universe. All things lie at His feet. She will be
adorned with glory and luster befitting her high calling. Upon
earth she loved Jesus, and out of love for Him went His way of
poverty, lowliness, obedience, and the cross. Now, in counter-
measure, she may reflect His glory (I Peter 4:13). What incom-
parable beauty, what regality will be seen in this Bride, whose
Bridegroom is the Lord of the world, the King of all Kings.

Yet she wears her crown only because Jesus won it for her in

His suffering. Therefore she takes off her crown again and again. Love compels her. She wants Him to have all the love and honor. He loved her so much that He redeemed her, and now she must love and thank Him with all her heart. And so there is a holy interplay in heaven. Could it be otherwise, where love rules? The Lord places crowns upon His Beloved, but out of love the crowns are taken off and cast before Him! It is a contest of love: the King and Bridegroom will honor His Bride, and serve her at the heavenly supper (Luke 12:37). The Bride glows with a reverent love for her King, Saviour, and Bridegroom. She wants to give Him honor. She lays her crown at His feet, and sings the song of love and adoration (Revelation 4:10).

The heavenly hosts could well cheer at the humility and love of their Creator, as He girds Himself and serves His Bride at table in the heavenly banquet hall. They rejoice at the coronation of the Bride. Once she was a sinner, without God, but now more richly endowed with God's grace than they themselves. Indeed, it is written that Christians shall judge the angels (I Corinthians 6:3).

This life at the throne, which begins with the marriage, is truly "eternal life." It embraces everything in a holy completeness: rejoicing and singing, loving and being loved, resting in Him and ruling with Him over the nations (Revelation 2:26, 27), honored and showing honor. It leaves nothing out, this eternal life: consummate accomplishment and utter rest; keen self-awareness and total self-effacement; loud shouts of joy and quiet moments of love to linger close to His heart; citizenship and an everlasting home in the heavenly beauty of the city of God, and yet holy service for Him (Revelation 22:3) in the unnumbered rooms of Heaven, which the Apostle Paul said were divided into three great levels. Yes, an endless festival at the Marriage Supper of the Lamb in heaven, and working and

serving in His Kingdom—this is life, "eternal life." In it is a richness, variety, and diversity beyond compare. Yet this life has no hint of disharmony or drudgery. It comes forth from God, who is love, and therefore it carries with it a deep inner harmony. In the "City of Peace"—which is the meaning of "Jerusalem"—the Prince of Peace will reign. There one knows nothing but a life of peace and joy.

What has God prepared for those who love Him? An indescribable glory, which finds its fulfillment and high point in the Marriage Supper of the Lamb. The tribulations and disciplines which were a necessary preparation during our earthly life are not worthy of being compared with the high goal set before us. Even upon earth it is a high point when one comes to the day of marriage. But a marriage upon earth is only a type or shadow of the marriage which will be celebrated in Heaven. Here all things are colored by sin and incompleteness. But there a marriage will be celebrated free of any hint of suffering, sin, or disharmony through unfaithfulness and death—such a marriage will Jesus, the King and Bridegroom, celebrate with His Bride, in the fellowship of love. "Bride," then, is the one Church—and the members in it—who have come together out of all denominations, fellowships, and nations. They are the ones who have lived in wholehearted love toward Jesus and all brethren in Christ. These are called "a flock," "a bride," "a wife." They will all be permitted to sit at one table, united in love with their Lord and Bridegroom, and with one another.

Who is able to describe the glory of this Marriage Supper? It is a day of joy for Jesus and for all of heaven. We catch a hint of this with the shout of jubilation that resounds through heaven at the coming of this Day:

Hallelujah! For the Lord our God the Almighty reigns.
Let us rejoice and exult and give him the glory,
for the marriage of the Lamb has come,
and his Bride has made herself ready.
   —Revelation 19:6, 7

What a joy for the Father when He sees the fruit of His Son's suffering! The Bride—a company of sinners, yet now conformed to the image of the Son through His sacrificial death. What a joy for the Son: now He may present His Bride before the Father! In her He has achieved His purpose. He gave Himself up to death for this one group from among all His creatures. He set them free from the power of sin, in order that they might once again reflect the glory of the Creator. The Bible says that the trees will clap their hands, in praise to God, when His people are set free (Isaiah 55:12). How much more will all God's creatures in the heavenly realm join in the festal celebration! Songs of heavenly joy will ring out. All heaven will break into dancing, singing and bowing before Him who has brought this day to pass. They behold Him, the fountain of all beauty, the adornment of heaven itself, the joy of the Father and the Bride, the source of all love. He bears yet the wounds, which are the tokens of His love for us, and His suffering. By them He redeemed us. In the light of His glance, shall the bowing and kneeling and prostration before Him ever end?

The suffering love of Jesus is a miracle love. It has transformed men of hate into men of love. It has created a kingdom of love. It has won the victory. This is the meaning of the Marriage Supper of the Lamb. This love, which went to death for us, has been given all power and authority. It maintains its victory over a world of hate. And that victory began with the "first fruits," the company of the Bride.

All heaven lives in anticipation of the Marriage Supper of the Lamb. Then, finally, the full number will have been completed. The Church—His Body, His "Wife"—will come home. What a day, for Heaven and earth! For when the first fruits of the redeemed come home, other groups will follow (Romans 8:23, Revelation 20:6). The victory of love will spread to a wider sphere. Revelation 22 tells how the nations shall be healed, as they eat from the tree of life. We know that the whole creation groans, awaiting the redemption of the first fruits and the celebration of the Marriage Supper (Romans 8:19–22). But the nations, and mankind itself, also await that redemption. The Marriage Supper of the Lamb heralds the final union of love between God and men. Would we not expect that the flame of this fervent love spread into the whole universe? Yes, the Marriage Supper of the Lamb marks the beginning of a new era in the kingdom of God. For "the Lord God Almighty . . . hast taken [his] great power and begun to reign" (Revelation 11:17). Then, after the Millennium, the New Jerusalem will come down to earth. It is His Bride, made ready, and He will fill it with His splendor. Then will come a new Heaven and a new earth. God will dwell in the midst of it. He will rule in His Kingdom with great glory, together with this host who are invited to the Marriage Supper of the Lamb.

Therefore Jesus longs for the first fruits to come home. The others cannot share in the redemption until the Marriage Supper of the Lamb has taken place. Until they come home, He cannot establish His royal reign. Do we truly understand how much God waits and longs for the marriage of His Son—how much Jesus waits? It is the eager waiting of love. It can scarcely wait to be united with the beloved. It wants all men to receive help, and all children to come home to the Father's house. The father of the Prodigal Son waited longingly for the son's return; a bridegroom

waits with anticipation for the day of his marriage; even so, the eternal love of the Bridegroom Jesus awaits the Day of His Marriage.

Should not the Marriage Supper of the Lamb also be the focal point of our longing and striving? Ought not our love to Jesus cry out, "Even so, come soon, Lord Jesus! Let Thy Day appear! Let Thy love triumph! Let Thy joy be complete!" Do we sense how heaven is already preparing for this day? It is near!

Blessed is he who can stand before the Lord on that day. His "first love" did not grow cold; it imprinted itself into the marrow of his being. Blessed are those whom love prepared to enter into the Marriage Supper in the power of His redemption. "Joy" and "bliss" are words too meager to describe what these souls shall experience. Indescribable glory will enfold them, and "thou givest them drink from the river of thy delights" (Psalm 36:8).

Yes, they will be with Him forever. Through all eternity they will feast on this unspeakable glory. They will see His face; they will behold His form, and be satisfied (Psalm 17:15), the loveliest in heaven and upon earth, our Lord Jesus Christ. For this is what the Father has prepared for *Those Who Love Him!*

Those Who Love Him
Basilea Schlink

Founder, The Evangelical Sisterhood of Mary
Darmstadt, Germany, and
Phoenix, Arizona

Translated by
Larry Christenson

BETHANYHOUSE
Minneapolis, Minnesota